The Parent's
Little Book of Lists

DOs and DON'Ts
of Effective Parenting

Jane Bluestein, Ph.D.

Health Communications, Inc.
Deerfield Beach, Florida

www.hci-online.com

Library of Congress Cataloging-in-Publication Data

Bluestein, Jane.
    The parent's little book of lists : dos and don'ts of effective
parenting / Jane Bluestein.
        p.   cm.
    Includes bibliographical references and index.
    ISBN 1-55874-512-2 (trade paper)
    1. Parenting—United States—Handbooks, manuals, etc.
2. Parent and child—United States—Handbooks, manuals, etc.
3. Child rearing—United States—Handbooks, manuals, etc.
4. Child psychology—United States—Handbooks, manuals,
etc. I. Title.
HQ755.8.B63   1997
649'.1—dc21   97-29511
                                                        CIP

©1997 Jane Bluestein
ISBN 1-55874-512-2

Publisher: Health Communications, Inc.
                3201 S.W. 15th Street
                Deerfield Beach, Florida 33442-8190

Cover design by Andrea Perrine Brower

To Irv Bluestein,

Grace Tereszkiewicz

and Clare Landman.

You are missed.

Contents

Acknowledgments...xiii

Introduction xv

Part I: Character Building

Character Building 3

12 Ways to Be an Effective Mentor 5

12 Ways to Model Responsibility and Self-Discipline 7

 9 Characteristics of Responsible, Self-Managing
   Children...9

10 Ways to Encourage Responsibility, Independence
   and Self-Management 12

11 Things You Can Do to Build *Irresponsibility*
   in Your Child 15

15 Characteristics of Children at Risk 17

 7 Characteristics of Families of Kids at Risk 20

10 Dangers of Encouraging Obedience
   and People-Pleasing 22

14 Ways Parents Encourage People-Pleasing
    and Dependence 25

10 Ways to Encourage Your Child's Individuality 28

16 Ways to Model Courtesy 30

13 Ways to Model Respect 32

19 Ways to Build Environmental Consciousness 34

17 Ways to Build Tolerance, Compassion
    and Global Consciousness 36

15 Ways to Model and Teach Optimism 39

 8 Ways to Model and Teach Gratitude 41

15 Ways to Model Self-Care 43

Part II: Wheeling and Dealing: Motivation, Cooperation and Avoiding Power Struggles

Wheeling and Dealing: Motivation, Cooperation
    and Avoiding Power Struggles 49

14 Ways to Create a Win-Win Home Environment 51

 8 Reasons Kids Rebel 55

 6 Ways to Accommodate Your Child's Need for
    Control—Without Losing Control Yourself! 56

15 Negative or Hurtful Ways Kids Act Out
    Their Need for Power or Control 58

10 Reasons to Offer Choices or Negotiate
    Options with Your Child 60

5 Criteria for Making Something Negotiable 62

12 Things to Remember When You Offer
    Your Child Choices 64

5 Characteristics of a Good Boundary 67

11 Reasons to Use Boundaries..70

4 Ways in Which Boundaries Differ from
    Expectations 72

9 Things to Remember When Setting a Boundary 73

6 Reasons *Not* to Ask Why 77

5 Reasons for Using Promises Instead of Threats 79

18 Things to Remember About Motivation 81

Part III: Relationship Building and Getting Along (Emotional Safety)

Relationship Building and Getting Along
    (Emotional Safety) 89

9 Ways to Create Emotional Safety in
    Your Relationship with Your Child 91

13 Things Kids May Do to Create a Sense of
    Safety and Predictability in Their Lives 93

12 Reasons a Child May Want to Join a Gang 95

26 Stress-Producing Obstacles in Relationships.................96

22 of the Worst Things an Adult Ever
    Said to a Child..100

30 of the Best Things an Adult Ever
    Said to a Child...102

  8 Things to Remember About Saying "I Love You" 105

12 Ways to Increase Positivity in Your Interactions..........107

15 Things to Remember About Reinforcing
    Positive Behavior 110

Part IV: Skill Building, Learning and Personal Growth

Skill Building, Learning and Personal Growth.................117

14 Ways to Encourage a Lifelong Love of Learning........118

15 Ways to Accommodate Your Child's
    Success Needs 121

  8 Things to Do When Your Child Makes a Mistake 125

13 Ways to Build Decision-Making Skills........................127

19 Ways to Build Thinking Skills 130

23 Ways to Encourage Creativity and Imagination 135

10 Ways to Encourage an Appreciation for the Arts.........139

31 Ways to Develop Literacy and a Love of Reading 141

  9 Ways to Minimize Problems with Homework 145

17 Ways to Build Positive Relationships with
    Your Child's Teachers 148

18 Questions You Can Ask When Your Child Says
    "My Teacher Hates Me" 152

Part V: Problem Solving and Prevention

Problem Solving and Prevention.......................................157

6 Reasons Not to Give Your Child Advice......................159

9 Benefits of Asking Questions Instead of
   Giving Answers..161

11 Ways to Encourage Cooperation with Chores 163

3 Ways to Deal with a Messy Room...............................166

7 Choices You Can Offer at Bath Time...........................167

12 Ways to Avoid Problems at Bedtime...........................168

14 Ways to Help Your Child Deal with
   Monsters in the Closet 170

10 Things to Remember About Potty Training
   Your Child 173

16 Ways to Avoid Conflicts over Food 175

10 Ways to Minimize or Avoid Problems at the
   Grocery Store 179

11 Ways to Avoid Problems over Money or Buying 181

14 Ways to Encourage Positive Choices for
   Good Health and Safety 184

11 Ways to Create Success with Your Baby-Sitter 186

15 Ways to Minimize Conflicts on Car Trips 189

15 Ways to Drug-Proof Your Child...................................192

Part VI: Dealing with Feelings (Supportiveness)

Dealing with Feelings (Supportiveness) 197

  5 Reasons to Help Your Children Learn to Express
    Their Feelings in Healthy, Nondestructive Ways.........199

17 Ways to Make It Safe for Your Child to Have
   and Express Feelings...201

  9 Characteristics of Good Listeners.................................205

14 Ways to Respect Your Child's Reality 207

16 Things You Can Suggest to Help Your
   Child Let Out Anger Nondestructively 211

12 Things Never to Say When Your Child's
   Feelings Have Been Hurt 213

13 Ways to Help Your Child Deal with
   Death or Loss 215

17 Ways to Help Your Children Survive
   Your Divorce 218

Part VII: Healthy Parenting (Personal Issues and Self-Care)

Healthy Parenting (Personal Issues and Self-Care) 225

14 Ways to Become a More Conscious Parent 227

  9 Ways to Be More Proactive...230

  4 Ways to Avoid Operating on a Double Standard 232

18 Characteristics of Parents at Risk 234

 8 Ways to Deal with Your Child's Saying
    "I Hate You!"..237

10 Ways to Avoid Getting Hooked by Your
    Child's Misbehavior..239

 7 Ways You Can Constructively Deal with Your
    Child's Abusive or Obnoxious Behavior.....................241

13 Arguments for Not Hitting Your Child.........................243

 4 Ways to Manage Your Anger.......................................246

13 Questions That Can Help You Learn from a
    Conflict with Your Child 248

 9 Things You Can Say to Detach from
    Unsolicited Advice or Criticism About
    Your Parenting Skills..250

10 Things to Remember About Changing
    Family Dynamics 252

10 Ways to Respect Your Parents as Grandparents...........254

26 of the Best Things About Having
    Two-Year-Olds in Families 257

18 of the Best Things About Having a Teenager
    in the Family 261

10 Ways to Make More Time for Your Child 264

 6 Ways to Take More Time for Yourself 266

36 Things You Can Do to Feel Great!...............................268

Part VIII: Writing Your Own Lists

Things I've Said That I Want My Children
    to Remember Forever.......................................273

Things I Respect and Admire About My Children..........274

Things About My Parenting That I'm
    Really Proud Of 275

Things I Hope My Children Say About Me
    After I'm Gone...276

Ways I've Shown Love to My Children............................277

Things I've Done As Well As My Own Parents Did
    (in My Relationships with My Children)....................278

Things I've Done Even Better Than My
    Own Parents Did (in My Relationships
    with My Children)...279

Things I Hope My Children Have Learned from Me.......280

Things I've Done or Said That I Hope
    My Children Can Forgive 281

Things I Would Like to Change in My
    Relationships with My Children 282

Things I'm Willing to Change in My
    Own Behavior 283

Resources and Bibliography 285

Resource People 317

List Index 325

Subject Index..329

Acknowledgments

▼

In addition to the specific resource people and materials cited for their contributions in the reference section at the end of this book, I wish to acknowledge with great gratitude the hundreds of workshop participants who shared their ideas and experiences anonymously.

A few individuals deserve a special note of thanks. They include:

Lisa Cramer and Linda Sorenson, for reading through the very first draft of this book and for the suggestions and contributions they made, and for helping me hang in there when all these hundreds of bits of information threatened to overwhelm me.

Greta Bratovš and Elvira Medved, for helping me survey and interview workshop participants in my training sessions in Slovenia, and for translating the ideas and contributions we received.

Maurine Renville, M.Ed., M.S.W., for checking some of the principles and terminology for accuracy, clarity and psychological soundness, and for the remarkable healing work she does.

Bert Shapiro and Robert Low, for working with me through the initial incarnation of this book and for graciously releasing me to "grow" in another direction when it was appropriate to do so.

Judy Lawrence, S. J. Sanchez and Maya Sutton, three of the wisest women in my world, for their friendship, inspiration and encouragement.

Matthew Diener, for "getting" the vision and respecting the process.

Jerry Tereszkiewicz, an amazing husband and wonderful friend.

Introduction

▼

A Picture of Positive Parenting

Many years ago, on a trip to the Philadelphia Museum of Art, our class got to see several original Impressionist paintings. I remember our teacher pointing out how the images had been created by separate bits of color, and how these little dots and lines and strokes all came together to produce a picture. If you stood close enough, you could see interesting specks of color, pieces of information that looked nice but communicated nothing in particular until you stood back a bit and saw how they all worked together. The lists in this book likewise present bits of information: little dots, if you will, that work together to create a picture; in this case, a picture of positive, loving parent-child relationships.

In my work with parents—in my workshops and in my writing—I often include a short survey to determine whether or not we're all trying to paint the same picture. I'll ask the parents how strongly they agree with statements like the following: "I want my children to believe that I love them unconditionally, no matter what," "I want my kids to feel emotionally safe in their relationships with me," "I want my children to be able to think and make decisions, especially when I'm not there." "I want my kids to be strong and confident enough to resist peer pressure," "I want my children to cooperate and do what I ask," "I would prefer having win-win interactions to win-lose interactions."

Getting agreement on these goals has rarely been a problem. The hard part comes when we start to look at how we actually act in our relationships with kids— when we examine how our behaviors shape the nature of our relationships and how they contribute to the behaviors and beliefs that children develop.

Our relationships are products of a number of factors, not the least of which are the actions we bring to them. Just as certain colors and brush strokes will create particular images, moods and impressions for an artist, certain parenting beliefs and behaviors can encourage and support particular outcomes in the relationships parents create with their children. Often, the most familiar behaviors will take parents in entirely different directions than they would like to go. In some cases, their actions can actually make it *more* difficult for them to achieve their aims!

For example, it's difficult for children to feel loved unconditionally when love is most often expressed in association with certain behaviors, achievements or particular choices about their appearance. (I've heard some parents say, "Of course I love my children unconditionally. And I *really* love them unconditionally when they make the honor roll.") It's hard to feel emotionally safe in a home where parents use power, anger, disappointment or unhappiness to get kids to do what they want.

Often, the same parents who claim to want kids who can think and make decisions independently also want kids who immediately do what they are told. Many parents who want kids who can indeed "just say no" would be incensed if their kids ever just said no *to them.* And some parents who want to create win-win interactions are very uncomfortable with the notion of giving children choices other than "do it or else."

But we can't have it both ways. It's like wanting to lose weight while insisting, "But I *always* eat six doughnuts for breakfast!" Whenever our policies, our habits or our behavior patterns do not support our goals, we have two choices: We either change our behaviors (eat a healthier breakfast) or change our goals (quit wanting to lose weight).

In terms of parenting, let's say your goal is to increase cooperation and minimize conflict in your relationship with your kids, but at the end of the day, you notice that you seem to get exactly the opposite—a minimum of cooperation with maximum conflict. At this point, you've got a choice: You either give up your goals and accept things the way they are, or you change. If you want the relationship to change, the way you interact with your kids is going to have to be different somehow, with different thoughts and belief systems, different responses to their behavior, different ways of asking for what you want, different words, a different tone, a different attitude.

This process doesn't have to be quite as overwhelming as it sounds. Even the greatest transformations start with small changes, which is why I started looking at the "pieces" of the parent-child relationship that are easiest to change. I wanted to identify small, specific parenting behaviors, beliefs and attitudes that could alter the course of the relationship in a big way. The result is the following collection of lists: techniques and ideas, actual questions and statements you can use to help accomplish a particular goal, and loads of practical suggestions that can help you "paint" a picture of the kind of relationship you want.

If you find that your intentions include encouraging cooperation without relying on threats, nagging and punishment; if you hope to minimize conflict without constantly giving in or giving up; if you wish to build confidence, independence, resiliency, responsibility and decision-making skills in your kids; and if you want to create an atmosphere of mutual respect, love, trust and consideration, you'll find some terrific suggestions here. You'll discover bits and pieces to help bring your parenting attitudes and approaches more in line with what you're trying to accomplish, and to strengthen, validate and build on patterns you already have in place. If your parenting goals are significantly different from those mentioned above, you may want to read through the lists to get a sense of what an alternate "picture" could look like and why it would be well worth considering.

Where These Ideas Came From

From my earliest days as an educator, I've been curious about what "works" in relationships between adults and kids. To be sure, a number of items in these lists come from my own experiences and observations. To gain a broader view, I set out to determine what had worked for other adults from a wide variety of cultural, economic and educational backgrounds (in some instances requesting and receiving information through an interpreter).* I handed out surveys and polls in my classes and workshops, and received hundreds of creative, touching, practical ways to approach and prevent problems with kids—many of which would never have occurred to me otherwise. In certain instances, I relied upon interviews with friends, associates and a number of individuals I consider experts on related topics.

Their suggestions, ideas and experiences are noted in the lists. When a list item states that "one parent discovered" or "several parents noticed," I'm referring to these contributions, the majority of which I received anonymously from unsigned surveys or from people who did not wish to have their names included. While I have acknowledged individuals whose feedback I specifically sought, for the sake of readability I have used their contributions within the lists as well.

In addition to strategies they had used as adults, many of the ideas people shared came directly from their own childhood—experiences they remembered as well as the effects those experiences had on them. Certainly, many of the comments and ideas they shared conveyed happy childhood memories. However, several contributions clearly reflected painful (and often avoidable) events from their early lives. I'm convinced that the eagerness

---

* Including parents, stepparents, foster parents, adoptive parents, grandparents, educators, counselors, health-care providers and other caregivers.

with which so many people participated in this project reflects a desire to help parents become more aware not only of the choices they have, but also of the potential impact their comments and actions can have on the children in their lives.

Using These Lists

In evaluating contributions and ideas for these lists, I tried to provide information for parenting children of all ages, and to offer a variety of approaches in order to accommodate a variety of needs, budgets, preferences and personalities.

You don't have to try—or even agree with—every idea on every list. For example, I asked parents to share boundaries they used to encourage cooperation from their children and received a wide range of responses. These parents swore by the examples they shared, although many admitted that it took them a while to get comfortable with the idea of only washing clothes that had been put in the hamper, "closing" the kitchen after a certain time or leaving their children in charge of getting their books and homework assignments to school themselves.

Clearly, we only set boundaries we need to set. If you don't mind washing clothes *and* picking them up off the floor, then you don't need a boundary to increase hamper use. However, many parents found that until they set this boundary (and this was a very common example), they ended up nagging, scolding and criticizing, and they *still* ended up with both jobs! Boundary setting is a great alternative, but only if a boundary needs to be set and only if the parent is willing to follow through!

If you find that a particular suggestion—or even a particular list—is not applicable to the ages or developmental levels of your own kids, move on to one you think would better apply in your situation. Likewise, if a particular technique doesn't fit into your value system or your time or your budgetary constraints, look for a more suitable suggestion. Look for ways to make the principles and techniques described work for you and your children. (For example, you probably wouldn't spend much time explaining how to use a lawnmower to a two-year-old; however, your teenager may benefit greatly from such instruction, just as your toddler would benefit from instruction on using certain toys or avoiding certain safety hazards common in her world.) The ideas in these lists are not things you *should* or *must* do to accomplish a particular goal. They are simply strategies and concepts other families have found to be useful or helpful. Try techniques that fit the ages and needs of your children as well as your lifestyle, your goals and what feels comfortable to you. Add your own ideas as they occur to you. In the margins of this book, on sticky notes or even in a journal, jot down things you notice or techniques you try.

When I started brainstorming the topics I wanted to address in this book, I looked at a variety of issues that challenged parents to define their roles and goals when interacting with kids. Several lists examine somewhat abstract concepts (like power dynamics, feelings or responsibility). Other lists look at specific issues (such as homework, chores or monsters in the closet) as opportunities to apply more general principles in concrete, day-to-day situations.

Some list items are clarified or expanded further in other lists, and many concepts appear repeatedly in different forms throughout the book. The overlap is deliberate, intended to tie ideas together, connect concepts, create layers and patterns, and define the type of relationship in which cooperation has a chance to occur with a minimum of conflict. Additionally, many ideas are relevant to more than one list, and certain concepts are repeated to make sense to the parent who reads this book in bits and pieces, rather than studying it from cover to cover.

Because a number of parents had difficulty identifying their relationship goals, there are also lists that describe the kinds of kids most parents say they want, as well as the kind of home environments, beliefs and family dynamics that support—or undermine—the development of these characteristics. These lists create a context and definition for the kinds of relationships the other lists attempt to build. I believe these lists are essential, especially for parents who need an extra nudge to give up a few of their old behaviors, or for parents who are afraid that letting go of traditional, authoritarian control techniques will leave them at the mercy of uncontrollable and obnoxious children. These lists are also helpful for parents who know there may be a better way but aren't sure what that looks like, and for parents who didn't even realize they had a choice.

The problem with a book like this is that it can be very tempting to take the suggestions presented in the lists and use them out of context just because they seem like good ideas—focusing on the "dots" in isolation, rather than stepping back to see how they work together to create the picture. While I've seen some relationships turn around fairly quickly when parents make even the slightest shifts in their behaviors or attitudes, there's the danger of imagining that a few new tricks will bring about a quick fix. Of course, there will be times that you'll see immediate results, but keep in mind that building relationships, like creating a work of art, is a process that unfolds and develops over time.

Don't let the idea of improving your relationship

overwhelm you. If you've ever remodeled a house (or even cleaned one that was particularly dirty or cluttered), you know that the entire project, while daunting, can actually be broken down into a number of small, manageable processes that are easier to tackle. It's the same with relationships—even relationships with a history of conflict and no-win power struggles.

Start with something simple and watch what happens. Say "I love you" for no apparent reason, especially if your kids aren't used to hearing you express this sentiment. Communicate your unqualified appreciation for a kid you've been especially critical toward. Try changing a threat to a promise, asking for a particular behavior in a more positive way. Rather than looking for ways to react to problems and infractions, start thinking in terms of prevention. Maintain your commitment to a better relationship, and a lot of the little things will take care of themselves.

A Few Assumptions . . .

I'd be lying if I said I didn't have a bit of an agenda here. Yes, these lists are designed to take parents in a certain direction, precisely because I believe that certain directions are more constructive, more positive, more effective, more healthy and less stressful than others. Simply collecting parenting ideas without some framework or context would have made no sense to me, and the number of contradictions inherent in just throwing together a bag of tricks would have been confusing, if not downright dangerous.

Before we get to the lists themselves, let's troubleshoot a bit. For example, whenever we talk about change, it's natural to come up against some resistance. It's always easier to complain, to want someone else to change, or even to believe that change is impossible than it is to examine and alter our own actions. However, if you're reading this book, you're probably looking for some new ideas and are open to thinking about different ways to interact with kids. I applaud you. You're more likely to parent successfully when you are conscious and deliberate about the choices you make rather than simply (and automatically) imitating the patterns you learned from adults in your life as you grew up.

Beware of the tendency to give up when you've had a bad day, especially when you've said or done something hurtful or destructive. The fact that you even notice is a very big deal! Be patient and trust the process. For the most part, kids can be remarkably flexible and resilient. They change when we change, although this process may take some time. If you would like your relationship with your kids to improve, look for things you are willing to change in your own actions, attitudes and language. Things may get worse before they get better, but the very act of becoming more aware of how you interact with others is a huge step in personal growth and a cornerstone of building better relationships.

Also, watch your reaction to some of the ideas here. Sometimes the greater the resistance, the better an idea may serve you. It may be well worth your while to reconsider a particular idea to which you have had an initial negative reaction, or at least to explore why you're having a hard time with it. If a particular list seems to be going in an unusual or unfamiliar direction, check for a box at the end of the list—you may find additional information to explain the purpose of the ideas in the list or to tie in the suggestions to a larger context.

I have tried to present the list items in a format that would be readable and accessible. The biggest obstacle from a writing standpoint was the use of pronouns. When I started jotting down list items, I didn't pay particular attention to whether I used "child" or "children." In addition, some items that talked about a single child used "he" in later references; others used "she." Reading a list from beginning to end, I found that a lack of uniformity left me with a bit of literary whiplash. Therefore the original lists were revised. With a few possible exceptions, all items in a particular list will either be singular or plural; all singular lists will use either "he" or "she" throughout.

While it may be obvious that these choices were made to increase the ease with which a reader could move from one list item to another, I recognize that reading a list that refers to a single male child has the potential to alienate a parent of three girls. And I know that seeing item after item with the words "your children" may be distracting to a parent of a single child. It is my hope that regardless of your situation, the point of the list item will not be limited by the number of children mentioned or the gender of the pronouns used. Examples that use "she" also apply to boys; those with "they" will apply to a single child. I ask your indulgence here, and your flexibility as well.

Remember, the best solution to parenting problems is always prevention—preventing the problem from continuing, from getting worse, from turning into other problems or from happening at all—even if that means backing up, looking at what in the relationship supports the problem (or created it in the first place) and making changes where they will do the most good—in the relationship itself. This book will help you fill your paint box with tools and colors you may never have tried before. I wish you great happiness and success in the lifelong development of your craft, and in the creation of your masterpiece—your relationship with your child.

PART I

Character Building

Character Building

Character traits such as responsibility, courtesy, respect and self-discipline do not develop in a vacuum. As a parent, you play an important role in the development of your child's character, not only as a role model, but also as a teacher or mentor. The following lists offer examples of things you can do to model (or demonstrate) these character traits as well as things you can do to teach them to or encourage them in your child.

To clarify the purpose of character development, some lists describe children who have certain character traits. Other lists describe those who are at risk—vulnerable to problems such as peer pressure, low achievement or substance abuse, for example—children who would certainly benefit from greater strength of character. Still others describe the supportive behavior of caring adults who create an environment in which character strength can emerge.

12 Ways to Be an Effective Mentor

❖ Accept your child unconditionally, just the way she is. Begin with her wherever she is in her development. Remind yourself that she's "right on schedule!"

❖ Appreciate her uniqueness. Give her space to go in different directions than you may have imagined or desired for her.

❖ Validate her reality or experience, even if it's different from yours. *(See "14 Ways to Respect Your Child's Reality" for more information.)*

❖ Enlarge her concept of the world and her understanding of how it works.

❖ Believe in her. Encourage her with love and faith (instead of threats, demands or derision) to help her achieve, confront her fears and go beyond her perceived capabilities.

❖ Support her need for emotional safety, some of which will come from the love and acceptance you offer, and some of which will come from the structure and limits you provide.

❖ Challenge her beliefs to expand her perception of possibilities for herself.

❖ Help her through a hard time by being there, by listening and by having faith in her ability to persevere and overcome adversity.

❖ Provide an outlet for her feelings without judging, advising or compromising her sense of safety.

❖ Help her discover hidden facets of herself. Widen the frame of her self-perception by helping her see herself beyond who she is now.

❖ Inspire an appreciation for new things. Light a fire with your own passion and appreciation for something that you enjoy or value.

❖ Demonstrate the kinds of behaviors and values you would like her to learn. Model virtues such as self-discipline, fairness, honesty, integrity and responsibility in your interactions with her and others.

12 Ways to Model Responsibility and Self-Discipline

❖ Return things on time and in the condition you borrowed them.

❖ Don't blame or make excuses; take responsibility for what you do and what you say.

❖ If you make a mistake, apologize and make it right.

❖ Change behaviors that are ineffective or destructive.

❖ Follow through on commitments. Do what you say you'll do and be where you say you'll be. When possible, deliver more than you promise.

❖ Pick up after yourself. Don't assume someone else will take care of it.

❖ Ask for what you want. Let people know what you want by communicating directly.

❖ Spend only what you can afford to spend.

❖ Deal directly with your child when a conflict arises between you and him. (Talking to a counselor or brainstorming with your spouse is very different from "Wait until your father gets home.")

❖ Model responsible language instead of "victim talk." For example, say "I don't want to do that" rather than "He won't let me"; "I made a bad choice" rather than "She made me . . ."; or "Please lower your voice when you talk to me" rather than "You make me so mad when you talk like that."

❖ Make choices based on your values and your child's needs, rather than deciding your actions based on how some other adult will react to your decision. Examine your need for someone else's approval or the need to avoid criticism or conflict.

❖ Keep your promises.

9 Characteristics of Responsible, Self-Managing Children

❖ Responsible children cooperate for some reason other than another person's reaction or approval, such as curiosity, the satisfaction of finishing, the joy of learning or doing something, or having access to a meaningful privilege or activity.

❖ Responsible, self-motivated children are far less vulnerable to things like peer pressure than conformers or "people-pleasers" (children who are motivated by approval). Although responsible children generally care what others think and will consider other people's feelings and needs, they can make decisions in their own best interests, even at the risk of ridicule or rejection.

❖ Responsible children consider their options, rather than just doing what they're told. They tend to cooperate more consciously than people-pleasers, considering various options rather than automatically making a choice to avoid conflict or a negative reaction from someone else.

❖ Responsible children are less likely to blame their choices on someone else. They may make bad choices, but it will usually be from a lack of experience or poor judgment.

❖ Responsible children have confidence in their own instincts and their ability to take care of themselves without putting themselves at risk, just to keep someone from making fun of them or abandoning them. They can understand and express personal needs, and believe they can influence and control their own lives.

❖ Responsible children can make the connection between their behavior and the consequences of their behavior. Negative outcomes are the result of their own choices, not someone else's fault.

❖ Responsible children tend to develop good decision-making skills because they have had practice seeing which options are available, predicting the outcomes of the choices they make, making choices and experiencing the consequences of their choices.

❖ Responsible children do not necessarily depend on authority to motivate them. They are more likely to ask questions and take some initiative than simply waiting to be told what to do.

❖ Responsible children may experience conflict between what they want and what someone else wants, but they can often negotiate win-win solutions and resolve this conflict without acting in negative or destructive ways.

10 Ways to Encourage Responsibility, Independence and Self-Management

❖ Communicate unconditional love and approval regardless of whether or not your child makes cooperative choices. Watch your attachment to specific outcomes. (In other words, don't offer choices hoping or expecting your child will pick the "right" one in order to get your approval.)

❖ Be a role model. Take personal responsibility for your own behavior and happiness. Be willing to change behaviors, beliefs and attitudes that do not work for you.

❖ Be generally more concerned with process (for example, how your child learns or makes decisions) than outcome (the actual results of your child's choices or behaviors). Try to keep your long-term objectives in mind, especially maintaining the quality of your relationship.

❖ Offer choices within limits you find acceptable. (This is a great way to encourage cooperation without resorting to threats or demands.)

❖ Trust your child's ability to make good decisions, even if you haven't had much evidence yet. Offer choices you know your child can handle. As she gains skill and confidence, widen the number or types of options you offer. Limit the number of choices you make *for* your child, even though you will often know what's best for her.

❖ State contingencies positively, promising positive outcomes "as soon as . . ." or "when you finish . . ."

❖ Keep your interactions reward-oriented. Start thinking of consequences as the *positive* outcomes of your child's cooperative behavior, good choices or remembering to do what she said she would.

❖ Respect your child's needs and desires. Even though you will have the final say in most situations, remember that her needs and feelings always matter.

❖ Examine why you feel threatened or insecure when your child demonstrates independence and initiative. Do whatever you can to deal with your feelings without interfering with your child's growth.

❖ Allow your child to experience the consequences of her poor choices (in non-life-threatening situations) in order to learn from them. Allow your child to take

responsibility for her own behavior and to change
behaviors that aren't working for her.

11 Things You Can Do to Build *Irresponsibility* in Your Child

❖ Lie for him.

❖ Make excuses for his behavior.

❖ Correct (or pay for) his mistakes for him.

❖ Model a lack of responsibility, commitment and follow-through yourself.

❖ Refuse to believe that he is capable of doing what he's been accused of doing.

❖ Fight his battles for him.

❖ Tolerate and excuse abusive or unacceptable behavior from him or others in order to avoid additional conflict.

❖ Be sloppy about holding him accountable for his behavior, especially if you're tired, frustrated or starting to wonder if it's worth the bother.

❖ Routinely let him get away with things if he has a good enough excuse.

❖ Do his chores and take on his responsibilities. Tell yourself it's easier to do it yourself.

❖ Let him have privileges even if he hasn't followed through on his commitments or what was required first. Use rationalizations like "Just this once" or "Okay, but this is the last time." Add "I really mean it this time" even though you don't.

It's natural to want to protect your child from the negative consequences of poor choices, to look for reasons to let him off the hook. Be careful because this tendency will ultimately interfere with his ability (or willingness) to take responsibility for his behavior. It's important to believe in your child without idealizing him, and also to recognize your value and importance in his life even when you aren't bailing him out or fixing his problems for him.

15 Characteristics of Children at Risk*

❖ They do not feel valued and secure, either in the family or in school.

❖ They do not feel "heard" or listened to. They do not believe their opinions are valued or important.

❖ They have difficulty predicting outcomes and thinking things through.

❖ They have a hard time seeing the connection between their choices and the outcomes or consequences of their choices.

❖ They have unrealistic expectations of themselves, others or situations.

❖ They lack a reasonable tolerance for frustration. They have difficulty taking no for an answer.

---

* At risk for problems such as vulnerability to peer pressure, early sexual activity, low school achievement, dropping out, substance abuse, compulsive behavior, pregnancy, depression, violence or suicide, for example.

❖ They have a high degree of despair, pessimism and negativity. They believe that they cannot realistically affect or change their lives for the better.

❖ They have a hard time expressing feelings constructively. They tend to "stuff" feelings or "blow up."

❖ They often have a hard time balancing consideration for others with consideration for self. They may either blame and avoid responsibility or act and feel overly responsible for other people. They have difficulty asking for help.

❖ They may have few interests (other than TV or video games). They rarely invite other kids to their homes.

❖ They may be perfectionistic, self-critical, reluctant to try new things and fearful of failure. They may become compulsively involved in projects and have a tendency toward overachievement. *Or* they may be reckless and seem indifferent, demonstrating poor school performance, dislike of school and poor attendance.

❖ They have difficulty thinking independently and can often be easily influenced or talked into things.

❖ They have friends who use drugs or alcohol, have favorable attitudes toward drug use, or experience early first use of drugs or alcohol.

❖ They lack a strong belief system.

❖ They rarely share their feelings and thoughts with anyone in the family.

All children will display some of these characteristics or behaviors from time to time, and many will not be at risk. However, if a number of these characteristics are present, particularly over a long period of time, children may be inclined to make self-defeating or destructive choices. The good news is that these characteristics can be turned around by loving (and patient) adults, safe and structured environments, and opportunities to learn and practice more constructive behaviors.

7 Characteristics of Families of Kids at Risk*

❖ Family pattern of verbal, physical, emotional or sexual abuse.

❖ Family history of substance abuse, addiction, compulsive behavior or co-dependency (behaviors that support or excuse substance abuse, addiction or compulsive behavior). Use of illegal drugs around kids. Heavy recreational drinking in the home.

❖ Family pattern of inconsistency or neglect. Lack of accountability to family for behaviors or whereabouts. *Or* overinvolvement and control of kids, lack of privacy, lack of boundaries with other family members.

❖ Family pattern of reactivity, rigidity, perfectionism, dishonesty, double standards, shaming, blaming, mistrust, disempowering, victimhood, intolerance, boundary violations, self-righteousness, denial or

---

* Family patterns and adult behaviors that put children at risk may include some or all of those listed. (*See "15 Characteristics of Children at Risk" for more information.*)

enabling (failing to hold a person accountable for that person's behavior).

❖ Family pattern of dismissing feelings, distracting or rescuing kids from their feelings, or using kids' feelings as an excuse for shaming, ridicule or making kids wrong.

❖ Infrequent or inconsistent expressions of love and acceptance. Conditional love based on appearance, achievement, social competence, performance or how well kids take care of adults' needs. Lack of emphasis on the unconditional worth of kids.

❖ Infrequent expressions of recognition, validation, acknowledgment. Recognition usually linked to effect of kids' behavior on parents. Praise expressed to manipulate and control.

10 Dangers of Encouraging Obedience and People-Pleasing

❖ People-pleasers are motivated by external factors, such as the need for outside (and usually conditional) approval. They often do what others want in order to feel safe, worthwhile or valued (for example, "so my friends will like me more").

❖ People-pleasers do what others want, to avoid disapproval, punishment, ridicule or abandonment, or for fear of hurting, disappointing or angering someone else. Their decisions rely heavily on another person's anticipated reaction.

❖ People-pleasers may obey anyone who appears to be important, powerful or popular. They tend to be highly influenced by peer pressure. They are far more vulnerable than other children to adults who may not have these children's best interests in mind.

❖ People-pleasers have a hard time saying no, even when saying yes would be unwise, inconvenient or even unsafe for them. Their negotiation skills are limited.

❖ Obedient children have a hard time seeing the connection between their behavior and the consequences of their behavior. Their sense of responsibility may be limited: "He made me do it," "Everyone else was doing it," "She started it."

❖ Obedient children are likely to blame their choices on someone else. They don't have to take responsibility for their choices (or how their lives turn out) because they were just doing what someone else told them to do.

❖ Obedient children may have a hard time functioning in the absence of authority. They lack initiative and would just as soon wait for someone to tell them what to do. They often depend on others to make decisions for them or make their choices simply to impress someone else.

❖ Obedient children believe that their ability to influence or control their lives depends on their ability to keep others happy, even if doing so inconveniences them, compromises their boundaries or principles, or jeopardizes their safety.

❖ When people-pleasers experience conflict between what they want and what someone else wants, they may express this conflict as compliance, guilt, passive-aggressiveness, resentment, helplessness or victimization.

❖ People-pleasers lack confidence in their own instincts and the ability to act in their own self-interests. They have difficulty understanding or expressing personal needs, or asking directly for what they want.

In the context of this book, the word "obedience" refers to the notion of simply doing what one is told, usually without evaluating the request, in order to avoid disapproval, rejection, abandonment or some other negative, hurtful or punitive outcome. Contrast obedience with "cooperation," which will look about the same in terms of how the child is acting, but which is motivated by something besides the reaction or approval of another person. Our real goal in building responsibility is encouraging cooperation, not obedience. In doing so, we can achieve the same behavior results without compromising the child's emotional safety or ability to act on his own behalf.

14 Ways Parents Encourage People-Pleasing and Dependence*

❖ They discourage decision-making and rarely offer choices (other than "do it or else"). Instead, they get what they want by making demands, ordering or telling. They tend to be authoritarian, critical and judgmental.

❖ They communicate conditional love and approval for "doing what you're told."

❖ Their happiness, pride and peace of mind depend on their children making the "right" choices. They use their reactions and feelings to control: "I'm so disappointed that you didn't make the honor roll," "I'm so happy when you clean your room," "I work so hard all day, and this is the thanks I get."

❖ They focus on immediate and short-term goals, often at the expense of long-term outcomes. They assume that their relationship with their children will somehow remain (or become) close and loving regardless of how they behave.

---

* And discourage independence and self-management.

❖ They mistrust their children's ability to make good decisions. They make most decisions for their children: "I know what's best for you."

❖ They state contingencies negatively, threatening that "if you don't . . ."

❖ They keep their interactions punishment oriented, focusing on the negative outcomes of their children's misbehavior, poor choices or forgetfulness.

❖ They discount, ignore or fail to respect their children's needs: "My house, my rules."

❖ They feel threatened by their children's independence, initiative, creativity, individuality or thinking skills. They may discourage, undermine or prevent these characteristics and behaviors.

❖ They protect their children from the negative consequences of their poor choices. They take responsibility for solving their children's problems or make excuses for their children's behavior.

❖ They do things for their children that the children are capable of doing themselves.

❖ They're uncomfortable seeing their children struggle and often jump in to "help" before their children have a chance to fully explore possibilities or figure something out.

❖ They reward dependence, self-sacrifice or devotion to serving the parents' needs (or the needs of others).

❖ They believe that their role is to teach their children *what* to think (rather than *how* to think) and count on their children to do as they've been told when adults are not around, even at the risk of peer rejection or disapproval.

All parents will display some of these behaviors from time to time—they are certainly familiar and, in many cases, may be fairly automatic. Occasional lapses will not put children at risk. However, if the tendencies listed above describe the way you frequently act with your children, you may be creating unnecessary obstacles to the development of their self-management skills. *(See "10 Ways to Encourage Responsibility, Independence and Self-Management" for more positive alternatives.)*

> "I don't know the key to success, but the key to failure is trying to please everybody."
>
> —**Bill Cosby**
> actor

10 Ways to Encourage Your Child's Individuality

❖ Don't compare her to anyone else, including your-self, her siblings, the neighbors or other children her age.

❖ Accept that she may like many things that you don't, and that she may hate things you really value and like. Remember that these differences are among the many things that make her special.

❖ Make a list of your child's talents, preferences and best attributes. Add to this profile whenever possible.

❖ Difficult as it may be, drop your agenda for who (or what) you want this child to be (or become). Accept your child for who she is and was meant to be.

❖ Examine *your* attachment to her appearance, inter-ests, preferences and goals. (To what extent do you need her to look or be a certain way so that you feel competent as a parent or validated as a person? To what extent are you embarrassed by—or apologetic for—the choices she makes?)

❖ Encourage her attempts to explore her identity, even though it may seem to take her in some strange directions sometimes.

❖ Quit worrying about what the neighbors (or your in-laws) are saying.

❖ Let her select and wear her own clothes. (If she's young or has a hard time making decisions, you may want to limit the choices to "either of these two sweaters" or "any T-shirt in this drawer.")

❖ Support and encourage her individual interests. Respect the fact that she may lose interest or change her mind as she explores different things.

❖ Remember that today's identity may soon be yesterday's experiment.

Remember that your child needs and deserves love, acceptance and respect regardless of what she does with her hair, who she wants to date or which career she wishes to pursue. (Minimize her need to act out for power or attention by allowing her to meet those needs in positive, healthy and constructive ways.)

16 Ways to Model Courtesy

❖ Say "please" and "thank you" in your interactions with others, including your interactions with children.

❖ Don't interrupt when someone else is talking. If you have to cut in, say "Excuse me," whether the person speaking is an adult or a child.

❖ Don't talk in movie theaters while the movie is on.

❖ Let someone pull out in front of you when you're driving (and acknowledge similar courtesies extended to you).

❖ Cover your nose and mouth when you sneeze or cough.

❖ Chew with your mouth closed. If you have something to say, swallow first!

❖ Never litter.

❖ Pick up after your dog on walks.

❖ Clear your table at fast-food restaurants after you finish eating.

❖ Knock before you open a closed door.

❖ Put the seat down.

❖ Hold a door open for someone.

❖ Offer your seat on a bus or train to someone who may need it.

❖ Write thank-you notes to acknowledge gifts or kindnesses. Make a point of letting people know you appreciate them.

❖ If you chew gum, chew quietly. When you're finished chewing, wrap your gum and throw it in the trash.

❖ Be considerate of people's allergies and sensitivities with regard to things like smoke, perfume, food, noise, environmental toxins, paint, exhaust or caffeine, even if these things don't bother you.

Modeling a behavior you want from your child teaches that behavior far more effectively than simply *telling* him to do it. Also, if you do these things consistently, your request that your child do the same comes across as much more reasonable!

13 Ways to Model Respect

❖ Listen. Make eye contact when your child is talking to you.

❖ Knock before entering your child's room, especially if the door is closed.

❖ Use language, words and a tone of voice that would be acceptable to you if your child were speaking to you.

❖ Value your child's need for fun and the time he spends with his friends.

❖ Give your child space to have different opinions and preferences from you (or other members of the family).

❖ Value your child's need for privacy. Don't open his mail or listen in on his phone conversations.

❖ Ask before using or borrowing something of his.

❖ If your child is struggling with something and is in no danger of getting hurt, hurting anyone or ruining something valuable, ask him if he wants help before you step in and do something for him.

❖ Allow your child to respond to situations differently from the way you would, without criticizing, shaming or ridiculing him.

❖ Stop tickling or teasing when your child asks you to—immediately and without comment, ridicule or judgment.

❖ Call your child what he wishes to be called. Resist calling him names or nicknames that embarrass him, or names he feels he has outgrown.

❖ When someone asks your child a question, let your child answer for himself. Resist the temptation to speak for your child, especially when he is present.

❖ Introduce your child when you encounter someone who hasn't met him. When you meet a grown-up friend who has a child along, be sure to say hello to the child as well as the adult.

19 Ways to Build Environmental Consciousness

❖ Minimize waste. Recycle and conserve as much as possible.

❖ Reuse boxes and shopping bags. Take your own bags to the grocery store.

❖ Help develop a recycling program at your place of worship or your kid's school.

❖ Landscape your yard for birds or wildlife. Build a birdhouse and feed the birds.

❖ Notice nature around you. Watch a sunrise or sunset. Look for animals or special shapes in clouds. Climb a tree and get a bird's-eye view of the world. Take a walk and look for different-colored flowers.

❖ Plant a garden, giving your kid her own plot. Participate in a community garden.

❖ Minimize the use of pesticides or chemicals in your home and yard.

❖ Look for and buy products in environment-friendly packaging.

❖ Start a rock collection.

❖ Dispose of motor oil, batteries and other damaging or hazardous materials properly.

❖ Plant a seed or a tree and watch it grow.

❖ Turn the water off while you're brushing your teeth.

❖ Help clean up parks or neighborhood streets.

❖ Carpool with friends. Instead of using a car, walk or ride a bike on occasion.

❖ Wrap presents in foil or the Sunday comics (both of which you can recycle).

❖ Start a compost pile.

❖ Grow your own herbs or vegetables.

❖ Do arts and crafts projects using materials from nature or saved from the trash.

❖ Suggest (or require) that a portion of your kid's TV choices be devoted to shows on nature, science or the environment.

17 Ways to Build Tolerance, Compassion and Global Consciousness

❖ Tell stories about your own family's cultural history. Explore your family tree. Encourage your child to talk to older relatives about what it was like when they were children. Create and practice your own family rituals.

❖ If you speak a second language, use it and teach it to your child. Encourage your child to learn other languages (including sign language).

❖ Visit and participate in a religious service that is different from your own.

❖ Participate, with your child, in a community service program. Volunteer together at a hospital, retirement community, homeless shelter, soup kitchen or animal shelter, for example. Help someone in need.

❖ Encourage your child to correspond with pen pals from different parts of the country or world.

❖ Try or make foods from different countries.

❖ Share a family tradition with someone from a different culture or religious background. Participate in someone else's family traditions or rituals.

❖ Answer questions honestly if your child notices or comments on someone's handicap or disability. Help your child understand special needs different people may have.

❖ Point out construction features (such as ramps, push-button door openers or braille signs in elevators) that make it easier for people with special needs.

❖ Notice places that are not handicapped-friendly. Ask your child to imagine how he would get around a particular place if he were in a wheelchair, for example.

❖ Find places that you see on TV (or in the newspaper) on the map or globe. Look on a map to find where different products come from.

❖ Read books, watch videos or search the Internet for information about different cultures, customs and religions.

❖ Read newspaper and magazine articles about things that are happening in other countries. Ask your child how his life would be different if he lived in those places and how he thinks the children living there might feel. (Reassure your child of his own safety if he seems to feel frightened or threatened.)

❖ Discuss the impact or potential impact of different global events (social, political or environmental) on your future.

❖ Attend arts programs (featuring dance, music, theater, crafts or other visual arts) from other countries.

❖ When your child is old enough, explore and discuss the impact of fear and hate throughout history. Read books or watch films that describe events in which people were denied rights, hurt or killed because of their racial, religious or political background, gender, or nationality. Talk about ways to promote love, tolerance and understanding.

❖ Pay attention to your language and any tendency to stereotype people by race, gender, physical characteristics, religion or nationality. Learn to see people with your heart.

15 Ways to Model and Teach Optimism

❖ Expect the best for yourself and others.

❖ Set goals for yourself and work toward them.

❖ Keep a clear, detailed picture of your goal in your mind. Focus on what you want, rather than on avoiding what you *don't* want.

❖ Help your child set goals and identify ways to reach them. Respect her dreams, even if they seem impossible.

❖ Practice and encourage persistence.

❖ Watch how often you express negative or pessimistic thoughts, or have negative expectations. (For example, do you say something like "It figures!" when something bad happens?)

❖ Look for the good that can come out of bad experiences. Help your child see how sometimes disappointments only mean that something better is coming.

- ❖ Maintain a mental picture of the world (and your life) as a place of infinite, positive possibilities, even better than you can imagine.

- ❖ Fight fear with faith.

- ❖ Develop "an attitude of gratitude." *(See "8 Ways to Model and Teach Gratitude" for more information.)*

- ❖ Keep your thoughts positive. Notice and acknowledge when you slip into fear, doubt and negativity. Make a deliberate effort to switch to more positive feelings and thoughts.

- ❖ Minimize the amount of time you spend with negative or pessimistic people. If possible, avoid them altogether.

- ❖ Make a deliberate effort to eliminate doubt and cynicism. They really don't protect you from much of anything. (Try "Well, why not?" instead.)

- ❖ Minimize your exposure to negative or pessimistic information, news and literature. Seek out positive, uplifting resources and read or listen to them regularly.

- ❖ Understand that pessimism, negativity and "scarcity thinking" are all learned traits. They can be unlearned and replaced with more constructive alternatives.

8 Ways to Model and Teach Gratitude

❖ Enjoy the beauty, richness, love and opportunities that already exist in your life.

❖ Express appreciation to people who do nice things for you. (Even if you receive a gift you don't particularly like, you can still acknowledge the positive qualities of the gift and the thoughtfulness of the giver.)

❖ Reframe painful or disappointing events as opportunities for growth and learning. Deliberately look for silver linings!

❖ Become aware of how much of your thoughts and conversation are devoted to complaints, how much of your focus is on what is lacking in your life.

❖ Be an example of happiness, abundance and appreciation. Watch out for tendencies to minimize or apologize for the good in your life, either to protect someone less fortunate or out of fear of attracting misfortune. Living small serves no one.

❖ If you don't already have one, start a personal gratitude journal. End your day writing down at least three things you felt grateful for that day.

❖ Create a family gratitude journal. Encourage everyone in the family to write, draw or dictate at least one contribution a week. (If weekly participation is impractical at this point, try this activity on birthdays or holidays, or even once a year, perhaps during the week before Thanksgiving or New Year's Day.)

❖ Let your child know that you are grateful to have him in your life—and why! *(See "30 of the Best Things an Adult Ever Said to a Child" for some ideas.)*

A note of caution: Gratitude is a very personal experience. Watch the tendency to tell others what they *should* feel grateful for. (Having much to be thankful for does not diminish the reality of sadness or disappointment, or the need to feel those feelings from time to time.)

Also, the idea of gratitude may be difficult for children (especially young children) to appreciate, demonstrate or even understand. Rather than punish ingratitude, help your child to learn behaviors that express gratitude and to develop this value as he grows.

15 Ways to Model Self-Care*

❖ Demonstrate a commitment to continual personal growth by learning new things and changing nonconstructive patterns in your own behavior.

❖ Make choices in the best interests of your own physical and mental health.

❖ Set, express and maintain your boundaries.

❖ Don't say yes when you want to say no. If it's hard for you to stand up for yourself, examine your own need for approval and your willingness to opt for self-sacrifice in order to avoid conflict.

❖ Take responsibility for your own needs. Quit waiting around for people to read your mind and take care of you. Ask for what you want.

❖ Make time for yourself—*just* for yourself!

❖ *Play!* Be spontaneous. Laugh. Create. Have fun.

---

* This term refers to your willingness to value and take care of yourself, personally and in relationships with others.

❖ Don't sweat the small stuff. Learn what to accept and when to let go.

❖ Delegate. (It is *not* easier to just do it yourself!)

❖ Watch out for perfectionism. Make sure that the standards and expectations you hold for yourself are fair and reasonable. If you make a mistake, instead of beating yourself up, focus on solutions and more effective strategies you can use the next time a similar situation presents itself.

❖ Develop a strong support network—people who will love and accept you no matter what, people you can go to when you're frustrated, angry, afraid or even doubting your sanity! Reach out as necessary.

❖ Limit contact with negative, critical, nonsupportive and nonaccepting people (even if they're related to you!).

❖ Refuse to accept, allow or excuse abusive language or behavior that is directed at you. Let others know how you wish to be treated. If necessary, walk away until they are willing to comply.

❖ Read or listen to inspiring material. Listen to music with positive, uplifting lyrics.

❖ Do nice things for yourself from time to time. Understand that practicing self-care is *not* the same as being selfish! (Selfishness either fails to consider the needs of others or simply disregards them. This is not the case with self-caring behavior.)

Self-care involves meeting your own physical, emotional, spiritual and psychological needs. It reduces the chances for you to feel resentful or disempowered in your relationships and enhances the quality of love and care you can give others.

PART II

Wheeling and Dealing: Motivation, Cooperation and Avoiding Power Struggles

Wheeling and Dealing: Motivation, Cooperation and Avoiding Power Struggles

This is probably my favorite topic because it offers some simple solutions to the power issues that drive parents crazy. The ideas that follow will paint a picture of an authority relationship that does not depend on disempowering or controlling your kid in order for you to stay "in charge." These are the ways you can accommodate your kid's need for autonomy and control within limits you find acceptable, without giving in and without giving up your own power.

These are the lists that will most effectively help you deal with the resistance you run into when you try to get your kid to do things he doesn't particularly want to do. Rather than simply showing you how to get what you want, these lists will help you build the kind of parenting skills that create a "win-win" environment in which your kid doesn't need to resist or fight you to get his power needs met, in which he cooperates because he's part of a team and because his cooperation is a way for him to get what *he* wants by doing what *you* want.

These lists also present ideas that are probably the most different from traditional authority relationships—the ones most of us grew up with—where kids are motivated by a need to avoid being punished, spanked, yelled at, grounded or shamed, or experiencing some other negative reinforcement, even a parent's disappointment. So, yes, some of these ideas may sound strange, even permissive, at first. I assure you, this is not the case. (Permissiveness, or a lack of limits, compromises a kid's security and safety needs.) So check these lists out. *Try* them out. You'll be surprised at how far a little empowerment and negotiation will take you. In addition to building important character skills like self-management, problem solving and personal accountability, the process won't cost you—or your authority—a thing!

14 Ways to Create a Win-Win Home Environment

❖ Focus on prevention rather than reaction. Start thinking in terms of "What can I do to encourage this desirable behavior?" instead of "What do I do when my child misbehaves?"

❖ Use your authority to set limits and offer choices. Decide and communicate what is and is not negotiable. *(See "5 Criteria for Making Something Negotiable" for more information.)*

❖ Accept the fact that a developmentally normal, healthy child has a need for varying degrees of power and autonomy at different stages of her life (usually beginning at about two years of age).

❖ Be willing to meet your child's needs for power or control within limits that do not disempower yourself or others. Emphasize goals, options, choices, solutions and *positive* consequences to reduce power struggles. *(See "6 Ways to Accommodate Your Child's Need for Control—Without Losing Control Yourself!" for more information.)*

❖ Allow and encourage your child to make her own decisions about certain things that are important to her. Having choices (within limits) creates a sense of control and helps build self-management and decision-making skills. *(See "12 Things to Remember When You Offer Your Child Choices" for more information.)*

❖ Invite your child's input and suggestions in determining policies or in planning events that will affect her life. Consider her feedback to whatever degree you can when making your final determinations.

❖ When setting limits or determining which options to make available to your child, consider her needs and preferences as well as your own. Use boundaries to attempt to accommodate everyone concerned. *(See "5 Characteristics of a Good Boundary," "11 Reasons to Use Boundaries," "4 Ways in Which Boundaries Differ from Expectations" and "9 Things to Remember When Setting a Boundary" for more information.)*

❖ Look for ways to meet both your needs and your child's. Ask her to propose solutions that will work for everyone or that everyone can live with. Develop a habit of asking "How can we *both* get what we want?"

❖ Use promises rather than threats. *(See "5 Reasons for Using Promises Instead of Threats" for more information.)*

❖ As much as possible, focus on long-term goals and processes (such as learning and development, decision making, thinking or planning) instead of immediate, short-term outcomes and results (such as actual choices or specific behaviors).

❖ Minimize acting out by meeting your child's needs for love, limits, attention, acceptance, power, success, belonging and safety in healthy, constructive ways.

❖ Look for ways to motivate cooperative behavior without using power, threats, humiliation or conditional approval. *(See "10 Ways to Encourage Responsibility, Independence and Self-Management" and "18 Things to Remember About Motivation" for more information.)*

❖ Encourage cooperation by following through on your boundaries (for example, withholding privileges and positive outcomes until your child does her part) rather than yelling, punishing or hitting.

❖ Examine your need to win, your need to be right or your need to control others. Look for ways to win without making others lose, ways to be right without making others wrong and ways to maintain control without robbing others of their dignity or autonomy.

"Win-win" authority relationships are typically far less stressful and destructive than "win-lose relationships." Therefore, all of the lists that address power dynamics offer suggestions that consider both the needs of the parent and the needs of the child (and the rest of the household), while respecting the authority of the parent.

---

8 Reasons Kids Rebel*

❖ To get control and power (autonomy).

❖ To prove you can't control them (independence).

❖ To get a reaction.

❖ To get revenge.

❖ To get peer approval (or peer respect).

❖ To get attention (even if it's negative).

❖ To self-protect. (To get you off their back or intimi-date you enough to stop bugging them.)

❖ To test your love.

All kids will test limits from time to time. However, kids growing up in win-win home environments rarely need to act out to create a sense of power, worth or safety in their lives.

---

* Includes fighting back, talking back, refusing to cooperate, deliberately doing something you don't want them to do or agreeing to do something they have no intention of doing just to be left alone. *(See "15 Negative or Hurtful Ways Kids Act Out Their Need for Power or Control" for more information.)*

6 Ways to Accommodate Your Child's Need for Control— Without Losing Control Yourself!

❖ Offer choices within limits you find acceptable.

❖ Ask for input and try to accommodate preferences when you can.

❖ Involve your child in family decisions, particularly those that affect him.

❖ Negotiate when you can be flexible. There are almost always things you can negotiate or compromise on, even within limits that may not be negotiable. *(See "10 Reasons to Offer Choices or Negotiate Options with Your Child" for more information.)*

❖ Offer your child different ways to reach the same goal. Or, if he doesn't want to do what you're asking, let him make you a counteroffer. If his suggestion is reasonable (like trading chores, doing something else you want him to do first or trying something a different way as long as it's still safe and potentially effective), give it a try. If his suggestion is unreasonable, let him know. ("That won't work for me" is far more respectful than "What! Are you crazy?") Ask him to try again, to find a solution that works for both of you, one you can both accept.

❖ To the degree that you are comfortable—and to the degree that he is capable—give your child full and exclusive responsibility for specific spaces (his room, a particular drawer or toy chest), activities (homework, bath time, free time from 3:30 until 4:30 each day) or other parts of his life (what to wear, whether or not he makes his bed, which friends to invite to his birthday party). Be willing to allow him to make his own choices and live with the consequences of the choices he makes in these areas.

15 Negative or Hurtful Ways Kids Act Out Their Need for Power or Control

❖ Saying no.

❖ Throwing a tantrum.

❖ Acting younger or more helpless than they actually are. Using baby talk long after they've learned to speak more maturely.

❖ Rebelling, fighting back, not listening (covering their ears, turning up the stereo).

❖ Being sarcastic, rude, contemptuous or verbally abusive.

❖ Being bossy or controlling with others, especially those younger or weaker than themselves. Bullying.

❖ Being aggressive with you or others.

❖ Refusing to eat. (Also, eating compulsively or self-destructively.)

❖ Swearing. Using offensive or violent language.

❖ Physically hurting you or someone else (a sibling, a smaller kid, an animal). Destroying property.

❖ Agreeing to do something and not following through, procrastinating, doing a poor or rushed job, "forgetting" or quitting before they finish.

❖ Threatening to hurt themselves (or actually hurting themselves).

❖ Deliberately failing or underperforming in an area they know is important to you (for example, refusing to be potty trained or getting poor grades in school).

❖ Exhibiting annoying, attention-getting behaviors, like whining or making noises.

❖ Accusing you of hating them or saying they hate you.

To meet your child's power needs without giving up your parental authority, give her choices, ask for her input and negotiate solutions that consider everyone's needs. Create as many opportunities as possible to give your kid control within limits you determine. Minimize the chance that she'll act out to get power in negative, hurtful ways. Also, make sure she has healthy and nondestructive outlets for her anger and frustration. *(See "16 Things You Can Suggest to Help Your Child Let Out Anger Nondestructively" for more information.)*

10 Reasons to Offer Choices or Negotiate Options with Your Child

❖ It minimizes power struggles and win-lose interactions.

❖ It generates commitment from your child and increases the likelihood of cooperative behavior.

❖ It allows you to make your boundaries and limits clear.

❖ It gives your child information about which options are available.

❖ It allows your child to have her wishes and preferences heard (even if you can't always accommodate them).

❖ It empowers your child by allowing her control within limits you determine.

❖ It models flexibility on your part.

❖ It builds responsibility and accountability by helping your child see the connection between her choices ("what I've done") and the outcomes ("what happens as a result of what I've done").

❖ It provides concrete evidence for your child that she has the power and ability to impact her own life. (This can minimize helplessness, despair and victim behavior.)

❖ Negotiating and decision making are critical "real world" skills to have in life, in work and in relationships (although these skills may get children into trouble with teachers or other adults who would just as soon have children simply "do as they're told").

5 Criteria for Making Something Negotiable

❖ If what your child wants (or wants to do) does not pose a threat to anyone's safety or health.

❖ If what your child wants (or wants to do) is not illegal.

❖ If what your child wants (or wants to do) does not inconvenience or create additional problems for anyone.

❖ If what your child wants (or wants to do) falls within the range of your acceptable limits. (That is, the desired option does not violate your family's rules or values.)

❖ If you have the time to consider what your child is asking for, or to offer choices and wait for a decision.

Many things in life are not negotiable. No matter how much you want to respect your child's wishes, you certainly don't let him play in traffic (it's unsafe) or strangle his brother when they argue (it's illegal and, presumably, contrary to your family's values). If your child wants to negotiate something that is absolutely out of the question—for any of the reasons above—acknowledge his desire ("I know you wish you could serve alcohol at your party") and offer choices within the realm of what actually *is* negotiable ("What would you like to serve instead?").

12 Things to Remember When You Offer Your Child Choices

❖ Be clear about what is and isn't negotiable.

❖ Keep the choices positive. Avoid choices that sound like "do it or else."

❖ Offer only acceptable options. Don't offer "good choices" and "bad choices" and hope your child pleases you by picking the right one. Also, don't ask your child whether he wants to do something unless it's okay for him to say no. (Are you really prepared to let him stay home from school when you ask him whether he wants to go?)

❖ Only offer options that are actually available.

❖ Keep choices simple at first. For a young child or an older child without much experience or confidence in decision making, offer only two or three options: "Do you want to wear blue or red socks with that?" "Would you prefer corn or peas?" "Which of these two television shows do you want to watch?"

❖ Increase the number of options available as your child gains confidence and experience.

❖ Follow a "no" statement with two "yes" statements, giving your child a choice between two positive options: "No grape juice in the living room. You can drink water in the living room or have your grape juice in the kitchen." Or "Stop! We don't hit people! You can hit the cushions on the chair or you can play with your brother nicely."

❖ If your child isn't crazy about the available options, ask him to suggest an alternative (one that fits within your goals, limits and budget).

❖ Allow and encourage input from your child.

❖ If your child has a hard time making up his mind, ask whether he wants you to decide for him. (That's a choice, too.) Don't be surprised, however, if he ends up wanting the opposite of whatever you pick. For a lot of children, that's part of learning how to make decisions. At this point, you can validate his decision ("Good choice!") and give him what he wants. If his choice is no longer available or there is no time to renegotiate what you've suggested, tell him he can "try again tomorrow (or later)."

❖ Tell your child how much time he has to decide (for example, "by lunchtime," "within five minutes," "until the big hand is on the six"). Tell him that after that, it's *your* choice.

❖ If he makes a choice he's not happy with, ask how
  he'll do it differently next time. (If there's time or
  resources, let him try an alternate choice.)

5 Characteristics of a
Good Boundary*

❖ *Clarity.* Boundaries are clear, specific and clearly communicated. They work best when you have your child's attention, when she understands what you're requesting, when the positive outcome of her cooperation is clear and when specific requirements, conditions or time factors are spelled out. For example, "I'll read you the next chapter in your story as long as you're in your pajamas with your teeth brushed by the time the big hand is on the six."

❖ *Win-win.* Boundaries respect and consider the needs of everyone involved. They attempt to create ways for both you and your child to get what you want. For example, "I'll be happy to drive you to the mall as soon as you finish your chores" or "I want to hear

---

* Boundaries are tools for building cooperation in relationships, for letting others know what you want and for letting them know which options are available to them (for getting what *they* want). Set boundaries when you want behaviors to change and wish to avoid negative, stressful behaviors such as nagging, yelling, threatening or punishing to get what you want. Whether you use boundaries in relationships with children or other adults, the characteristics of boundaries and dynamics of boundary setting are the same.

about your day. I'll be free to give you my full attention in 15 minutes."

❖ *Proactivity.* Boundaries work to *prevent* problems and are typically expressed *before* a problem occurs or before it is allowed to continue (or get worse). For example, "You can play my stereo as soon as you can demonstrate how to use it correctly (or replace the CD you damaged)." "When we go to the store, you can select one kind of cereal (or candy bar)."

❖ *Positivity.* The most effective boundaries typically focus on the positive outcomes of cooperation. They are also expressed positively, as promises rather than threats *(see "5 Reasons for Using Promises Instead of Threats"),* or simply as information (with the implication that the positive outcome is available, for example, until a certain time or under certain conditions). For instance, "If you put your dirty clothes in the hamper by 9:00 Saturday morning, I'll wash them for you" or "The kitchen closes at 8:00."

❖ *Follow-through.* Follow-through—allowing a positive consequence to occur only when your child does what you've asked—is what communicates that you mean what you say and you say what you mean. It increases the likelihood that your child will take you seriously when you ask for what you want, and it improves the chances that she will cooperate as well (if it's really the only way she can get what she wants).*

A simple example: A store that wishes to build positive relationships with the public opens at 7 A.M. and closes at midnight. The hours are *clearly* noted in their ads, on the door or over the phone if you call ahead, so you can find out *proactively,* before you go down there when they're not open. Their hours accommodate most schedules while closing long enough to clean up and restock *(win-win)*. As long as you get there on time, you get to shop and buy what you need *(positivity)*. And ordinarily, if you get there even a minute or two after midnight, the store will be closed *(follow-through),* even though you may have a perfectly reasonable excuse for being late!

---

* Boundaries allow you to follow through without even getting angry! Follow-through works wonders, but it requires patience, faith, consistency and courage!

11 Reasons to Use Boundaries

* Boundaries allow you to express your limits and to communicate the conditions or availability of certain privileges that your child desires.

* Boundaries prevent conflict and build win-win power structures. They help you take care of yourself while attempting to accommodate your child's needs or desires.

* Boundaries build a reward-oriented home environment. They emphasize positive consequences—desirable outcomes available with cooperation.

* Boundaries create less stress and fewer power struggles than rules and demands (which are typically win-lose and often focus on punishments or negative outcomes for noncompliance).

* Boundaries build mutual consideration and respect.

* Boundaries do not rely on your child's fear of your emotional reaction (such as anger or disapproval) to help you get what you want.

- Boundaries allow positive and negative consequences to occur in a nonpunitive environment (negative consequences simply being the *absence* of positive consequences). As long as you allow only positive consequences to occur when your child has done his part, boundaries hold your child accountable for his own behavior.

- Boundaries with good parental follow-through can minimize your child's whining, begging, temper tantrums or reliance on excuses to get what he wants.

- Boundaries leave the door open for your child to change his behavior in order to get his needs met. While rules or threats emphasize the penalties for misbehavior, boundaries focus on the ability to make more constructive choices.

- Boundaries do not threaten emotional safety in relationships.

- Boundary setting is especially effective in an atmosphere of love, acceptance and respect, and the process can help *create* these qualities in an otherwise troubled relationship.

4 Ways in Which Boundaries Differ from Expectations

❖ A boundary offers a positive outcome, connecting something you want to something your child wants. An expectation focuses exclusively on what you want.

❖ The commitment to an expectation is usually one-sided—from you, the parent. A boundary attempts to generate commitment from your child as well.

❖ Expectations can threaten your child's emotional safety. They motivate by connecting your child's behavior to your reaction: "I expect this" suggests disappointment, anger or punishment if your child doesn't fulfill your expectation. Boundaries connect your child's behavior to some outcome *unrelated* to your reaction. There is no stress on the relationship. The only thing at stake is the positive outcome.

❖ Expectations communicate your attachment to a particular outcome. Boundaries allow you to let go. With a boundary, you are less vulnerable to (or affected by) your child's choices.

9 Things to Remember When Setting a Boundary

❖ Use boundaries to let your child know your limits and tolerances, your availability, the conditions under which you will participate in some activity, which privileges are available or the conditions under which a privilege is available to your child. Use boundaries to give your child information she can use in making decisions.

❖ Using past experience (and common sense), anticipate what you will want and what your child will probably want as well. For example, will she probably ask you to buy her something if you take her to the store? What does she usually want? What are you willing to buy (or spend)? Consider both your needs and your child's needs when formulating your boundary.

❖ Be clear and specific about what you're asking for, what you would like, which options are available, the times or conditions under which a positive outcome is available, or any other factors that your child will need to know in making her choices or anticipating a particular event.

❖ Communicate your boundary *before* there is a conflict, or before the conflict continues or reoccurs: "You can pick out one candy bar at the checkout counter." "We're not buying any toys today." "If you want to get your homework in on time, you need to remember to take it to school yourself."

❖ State boundaries positively, as promises rather than threats: "You can watch the movie if your homework is done by 7:00" rather than "You're not watching the movie if your homework isn't done by 7:00." *(See "5 Reasons for Using Promises Instead of Threats" for more information.)*

❖ Be prepared to follow through. If you're not willing to withhold positive outcomes until your child does her part—whether it's finishing her homework, completing a chore, putting her plan in writing or toning down her voice—don't bother setting the boundary in the first place.

v Examine your attachment to particular outcomes. For example, if you are heavily invested in your child's success in school, you'll have a hard time following through on your decision to allow your child to be responsible for getting her homework, lunch money or permission slips to school on her own. Either refrain from setting this boundary (and don't complain when your child needs you to deliver her "stuff" for her) or use your resistance to following through as a chance to look at your need to protect your child (or yourself) from her forgetfulness.

❖ Watch the tendency to make excuses, give warnings or let things slide "just this once." This is a great way to teach your child that you don't really mean what you say and that it's okay to disrespect your boundaries. If you want to build in some flexibility, do so before your child blows it. (One parent let his son earn "bonus" cards by doing extra chores or making curfew a certain number of nights in a row. Then, if his son wanted to stay out an extra 15 minutes, he could trade in a card for the privilege ahead of time.)

❖ If your child is unable to perform or complete her end of the bargain because the request or time limit was truly unreasonable, because the instructions were not clear or understood, or because your child was developmentally incapable or lacked the necessary skill or experience to do what you wanted, it was a bad boundary. This is not the same as making excuses for a developmentally capable child who simply doesn't come through. In this instance, back up and try again (delaying the request until your child is more capable; setting a different boundary; or offering more clarity, instruction or a more reasonable time limit, for example). Do not withhold positive outcomes at this time.

6 Reasons *Not* to Ask Why*

❖ It focuses on excuses rather than commitment.

❖ It assumes your child knows why he did it (or forgot to) and can adequately explain his reasons to you.

❖ It suggests that your boundaries and limits are flexible if your child has a good enough excuse: "If you're creative (or pathetic) enough, you're off the hook."

❖ It puts you in the position of having to judge the "validity" of your child's excuses and arbitrarily decide whether or not to hold him accountable.

❖ If you have a good boundary with a positive outcome, if your child is developmentally able to do what you've asked and if he has had enough time, training or reminders to succeed, *why* doesn't matter—the positive outcome is simply not available until your child changes his behavior or fulfills his commitment.

---

* This title refers to not asking a child to explain why he did something wrong or forgot to do something he was supposed to do (or had agreed to do).

❖ Your child's answer may tempt you to attack or shame him ("You should have thought of that before," "You should have known better," "How could you have been so stupid?") instead of using the occasion as an opportunity for your child to make more responsible choices and correct his behavior.

Instead of looking for excuses or reasons for a misbehavior, help your child identify solutions, better ways to do it next time or ways he can correct his mistakes. This is not about rigidity—you can always check in with progress, give reminders or build in flexibility *before* your child makes an error or misses a deadline. This is about having the courage to let go, follow through, and use these events as opportunities for your child to learn and grow. (Remember, the movie will start at 8:00, the store will close at midnight and your taxes will be due on April 15 no matter *why* you're late.) As with anything else in life, there will always be judgment calls, but be aware that asking "why" or "why not" is a bad habit to get into if you truly wish to build responsibility and accountability in your child.

5 Reasons for Using Promises Instead of Threats*

❖ Promises create less stress in relationships because they're much easier and nicer to hear. (Say a contingency in your head, first as a threat and then as a promise. Which would make *you* feel more defensive, insulted or rebellious?)

❖ Promises offer your child some power in the situation, and demonstrate your intention and desire for your child's wants to be fulfilled. Both of these can minimize the need for resistance or rebelliousness.

❖ Promises focus on positive outcomes, which are "safer," less stressful motivators than avoiding negative outcomes or punishments.

❖ Promises do not compromise emotional safety (unless the positive outcome offers conditional love, approval or parental happiness, for example, if your child cooperates).

---

* For example, "If your chores are finished by 4:00, you can go out to play miniature golf" (promise) vs. "If your chores aren't done by 4:00, you cannot go out to play miniature golf" (threat). Both statements connect something the child wants (golf) to something the adult wants (chores done by a particular time).

❖ Promises make your child's behavior his responsibility: Positive consequences follow *only* when your child cooperates or follows through. In other words, it's up to him to do whatever is necessary to experience desirable outcomes. (One mother reported that her 16-year-old son was dismayed when she changed a former threat to "Of course you can use the phone for an hour—as long as your homework is finished by 8:00." The teen complained, "Yeah, but now if I can't use the phone, I can't blame *you!*")

18 Things to Remember
About Motivation

❖ There is no such thing as unmotivated behavior. Everything we do, we do to experience certain personal benefits (including the benefit of avoiding physical, emotional, spiritual, mental or financial discomfort or penalties).

❖ In the long run, positive consequences create less stress and protect the relationship better than fear of negative consequences.

❖ In every situation, we have choices. (Even "Do it or else!" gives us a choice!) We always make the choice that pays off best for us, the one that seems the most beneficial.*

❖ Even seemingly self-sacrificing choices are made in anticipation of some positive outcome, be it self-satisfaction, self-righteousness, congruence with

---

* From an adult's point of view, a kid's decision to become sexually active, for example, would probably not be the "most beneficial" choice. However, if the kid's priority is to avoid rejection, ridicule or abandonment, the decision will be based on determining which choice will be the most beneficial in accommodating *that* particular need.

personal values, the need for approval, the desire to obligate, or some other goal that has personal meaning.

❖ The likelihood of doing something for the pleasure of doing it (or even just because it needs to be done) increases when the task itself affords fun, success or a sense of satisfaction, maturity, autonomy or independence.

❖ Kids tend to be far more cooperative when their cooperation doesn't make them feel like they're "giving in" or being controlled or disempowered.

❖ Everyone requires "external" motivation for certain behaviors. Some kids, for example, will clean their room for the fun of cleaning or the privilege of running a vacuum cleaner. Others will need the external motivation of being able to find things, being able to get to the bathroom in the dark without tripping, having a place to play or do their homework, or being allowed to have friends over or go out to play after they're finished.

❖ Kids are more likely to do what you ask when the outcome or payoff is more need-fulfilling than avoiding the task you're asking them to do, when they're not competing with you for power and when certain privileges are only available after they have done what you've asked.

❖ Effective motivators must be meaningful to the kid you're trying to motivate. Telling your kid she can watch TV when she finishes a chore will only motivate her if she enjoys watching TV more than she enjoys *not* doing the chore.

❖ The best positive consequences are ones that don't depend on the reaction or approval of someone else. (Making choices to protect yourself against anger or rejection is very different from making choices to enjoy some positive outcome in an environment in which your safety, worth and acceptance are unconditional.) These kinds of motivators build responsibility and self-reliance rather than an overdependence on other people's opinions and reactions.

❖ Using guilt or shame to motivate is harmful and destructive.

❖ Stickers or tokens may be suitable for specific tasks like brushing teeth or for chore charts. However, activities and privileges are usually more effective and more meaningful, particularly (but not exclusively) with older kids.

❖ Giving your kid choices or a chance to negotiate may be all you need to generate her commitment. Sometimes, simply having some power in a situation is motivation enough.

❖ Certain positive outcomes may not be immediately meaningful. For example, getting her clothes washed may not motivate your kid to put her dirty laundry in the hamper until she can't find anything clean to wear.

❖ Watch the tendency to overmotivate (like giving your daughter $10 every time she runs the vacuum cleaner), or to motivate your kid to do tasks she already enjoys or is already in the habit of doing.

❖ Eventually, certain tasks become automatic and won't require continuous or external reinforcement or motivation.

❖ Motivators must be accessible. Some kids can work for months for a meaningful positive outcome. Other kids need more immediate and frequent reinforcement (at least in the beginning).

❖ The whole idea of motivating your kid will be a lot easier if you don't have a negative attitude about motivation and if you don't get hung up on the idea that motivation equals bribery. Any meaningful outcome—positive or negative—can be considered a bribe, whether we're talking about privileges, self-satisfaction, sense of accomplishment, or threats of punishment or conditional love and approval.* We all want to experience something positive (and avoid negative consequences) for the choices we make.

---

* "Do this, or I'll punish you" is just as much a bribe as "Clean out the garage, and then you can go out with your friends."

PART III

Relationship Building and Getting Along (Emotional Safety)

Relationship Building and Getting Along (Emotional Safety)

This entire book is devoted to building the relationship between you and your child, creating an atmosphere in which everything else can develop—from discipline and strength of character to good homework habits and cooperation when it comes to chores. Parents who experienced positive changes in their children's behavior reported that the improvements invariably started with changes in the relationship and in the general emotional climate of the household.

This section looks at ways to build the quality of the relationship—as well as the things that can get in the way. Some of the lists examine what can happen in children's lives when the emotional safety and predictability they need are not available to them. Other lists focus on words and language, positivity, reinforcement and appreciation, as even a tiny shift in these areas can ripple through the relationship at many levels.

9 Ways to Create Emotional Safety in Your Relationship with Your Child

❖ Love your child no matter what.

❖ Communicate your boundaries and limits clearly.

❖ When there is a conflict, attack the problem, *not* your child. Watch for put-downs, criticisms and judgments. (There's a big difference between "These counters are dirty" and "You are such a slob!")

❖ Give your child space to have his feelings, preferences and opinions, to be who he truly is. Accept your child and who he is unconditionally, even if his behavior is not acceptable.

❖ Listen without interrupting, judging or moralizing.

❖ Avoid backing your child into a corner. For example, don't ask him to choose between spending time with you and spending time with his friends, or demand that he agree with your preferences or opinions to get your approval.

❖ Follow through. Do what you say you'll do. (You provide structure, security and predictability when you quit making excuses for your child, giving warnings or caving in on your boundaries.)

❖ Use boundaries to request behaviors you want instead of messages that make your child responsible for your feelings or peace of mind: "I'll take you to the pool after your chores are finished" rather than "When you don't do your chores, I feel hurt (or angry or frustrated)."

❖ Communicate your feelings responsibly: "I'm angry (and need a few minutes to cool off)" instead of "You make me angry." Avoid using your feelings to control.

"Your contribution as an adult can be measured by the quality of your conversations with youth."

—**Sandi Redenbach, M.Ed.**
parent and teacher educator

13 Things Kids May Do to Create a Sense of Safety and Predictability in Their Lives*

❖ Comply, conform or people-please; doing things specifically to avoid rejection or abandonment.

❖ Quit caring. (Indifference can be a great insulator: "You can't hurt me if I don't care.")

❖ Withdraw or shut down. Isolate.

❖ Overachieve, overperform or seek perfection to gain approval or maintain a conditional sense of worth.

❖ Stay extremely busy or distracted.

❖ Underachieve. Deliberately perform below their capability to lower others' expectations of them.

❖ Get high, using some substance (drugs, alcohol, nicotine, food) or behavior (exercising, watching TV, playing video games, shopping, gambling to escape, becoming numb or stay distracted).

---

* Even though it may create other problems for them.

❖ Engage in "cutting" or self-mutilation, making internal pain external. (While this behavior would hardly seem to be a way to create safety, kids familiar with this practice report that it is comforting and tension-relieving. This behavior is much more common than many people realize.)

❖ Seek emotional safety and comfort outside the home through a relationship, early marriage or sexual activity.

❖ Rebel or deliberately alienate others: "Hurt them before they hurt you."

❖ Fail to make decisions or commitments. Let other people think and decide for them.

❖ Develop patterns of helplessness, dependence or even illness, to appeal to a parent's need to be needed *or* to minimize demands a parent might place on them.

❖ Agree to do something just to get someone off their back. Say yes despite having no intention of following through.

12 Reasons a Child May Want to Join a Gang

❖ Gangs offer acceptance.

❖ Gangs offer belonging (affiliation).

❖ Gangs offer fun.

❖ Gangs offer love.

❖ Gangs offer emotional safety.

❖ Gangs offer power (control, potency).

❖ Gangs offer identity.

❖ Gangs offer respect.

❖ Gangs offer modeling.

❖ Gangs offer recognition (attention).

❖ Gangs offer success (competence).

❖ Gangs offer structure (standards, limits).

Gangs tend to be less attractive to a child who gets these needs met at home or in school.

"The family has to be the better gang."

—**Louis Gonzales, Ph.D.**
violence prevention specialist

26 Stress-Producing Obstacles in Relationships

❖ Needing to be in charge or in control (especially when it depends on disempowering or controlling others, or when it disregards other people's desire for control and autonomy).

❖ Needing to be right (when it depends on others being wrong, when it requires that you make others wrong, or when it means that others must agree with you or support your views and actions).

❖ Needing to be needed or feel important (when it requires the dependence of others).

❖ Needing someone else to exhibit certain behaviors, appearance, values, preferences or abilities in order to feel good about yourself (or successful as a parent or spouse, for example).

❖ Expectations, especially when your preferences or desires are not communicated or agreed to before-hand. Having an agenda for how another person should be or behave: "I expected you to be home by now," "If you really loved me, you would have called," "I can't believe you didn't get me a card." (Typically, the only person committed to an expectation is the person who has the expectation.)

❖ Arrogance or self-righteousness. Assuming the other person understands or knows what you want: "Come home at a *reasonable* hour," "I was ready to leave two hours ago!" "I shouldn't have to tell you that."

❖ Assuming that others operate (or should operate) with your priorities and values: "How can you spend so much time at the mall (or watching football)?" "You shouldn't date someone from that part of town."

❖ Assuming that someone will think, feel, act or react in a certain way: "I didn't tell you because you'd get mad," "I didn't want to bother you," "I was afraid you'd be hurt." Thinking for another person.

❖ Tunnel vision. An inability to see the "big picture."

❖ All-or-nothing thinking (sometimes called dualism or black-and-white thinking). A tendency to think in terms of opposite extremes. An inability to see multiple options or other points of view.

❖ Fear of conflict, rejection or abandonment. Compromising personal values or standards, making decisions based on someone else's reaction or possible reaction.

❖ Denying that a problem exists or making excuses for someone else's unacceptable behavior, rather than confronting that person or asking for more reasonable behavior.

❖ Reactivity. Overreacting.

❖ Victim thinking. The perception of having no power to change a situation (or your thinking) for the better or to do things differently.

❖ Dependence on others for your own needs.* Abdicating personal responsibility. Being afraid or unwilling to let people know what you want.

❖ Projecting or blaming: "If you would shape up, there wouldn't be a problem."

❖ Double standards. Expecting or demanding behaviors from others that you do not model or demonstrate yourself.

❖ Criticizing, shaming, belittling, judging or any form of attack. Focusing on the negative (especially in someone else's behavior, choices, character or values).

---

* As opposed to healthy interdependence in relationships. Dependence refers to the belief that your needs, feelings or peace of mind are someone else's responsibility.

❖ Asking someone to defend or explain his behavior rather than asking for what you want: "Why did you borrow my sweater without asking me first?" instead of "I want you to ask before you borrow my things."

❖ Assuming that another person is committed to an agreement simply because you have expressed what you want. Not asking for agreement.

❖ Ignoring requests another person makes.

❖ Lack of consideration for another. Focusing on your own needs to the exclusion of others' needs. Failing to respect another person's boundaries, privacy or time.

❖ Taking someone for granted. Assuming another person will always be around.

❖ Focusing on another person's needs to the exclusion of your own. Discounting or dismissing your needs in favor of someone else's (when doing so will have a negative or harmful effect on you). Self-sacrifice.

❖ Resistance to being conscious and present in the relationship.

❖ Resistance to personal change: "I've always felt that way," "This is just the way I am (or do things)."

22 of the Worst Things an Adult Ever Said to a Child*

❖ "You'll never amount to anything."

❖ "I wish I'd never had you" or "We never wanted you."

❖ "How could you be so stupid?"

❖ "You're useless (or hopeless)."

❖ "I can't stand you."

❖ "If you don't straighten out, I'm going to commit you to the state hospital."

❖ "You'll never be college material."

❖ "You're lying."

❖ "You'll never be any good at that."

❖ "Why can't you be more like your brother (or sister)?"

❖ "You're fat and ugly."

---

* Personal recollections of adults surveyed for this book. Many examples were submitted by more than one person.

❖ "You have a terrible personality. Only a real idiot would ever like you."

❖ "Children should be seen and not heard."

❖ "You should be happy. This is the best time of your life."

❖ "Your mother and I wouldn't be getting divorced if it weren't for you."

❖ "We always liked your dad's first wife better than your mother. We wish he'd never married your mom."

❖ "If you do that, you're not my daughter."

❖ "You could have been somebody."

❖ "Do what I say, not what I do."

❖ "You are the shortest person in the class, so you'll be the last one to have your picture taken."

❖ "I'm sorry you didn't play, but we needed to win the game."

❖ "I love you, but . . ."

Whether a thoughtless comment or something cruel said in a moment of anger, our words take root and can live forever in the heart of a child.

Think before you speak.

30 of the Best Things an Adult Ever Said to a Child*

❖ "I love you."

❖ "How are you?"

❖ "You are a good person."

❖ "You can do anything you choose to do."

❖ "You're very smart."

❖ "I'm so glad we've got you."

❖ "You are very special (or terrific)."

❖ "When you make up your mind to do something, you always follow through."

❖ "You are number one."

❖ "Congratulations! You deserve this!"

❖ "You'll go far. I'll never have to worry about you."

---

* This list includes suggestions and personal recollections of adults surveyed for this book. Many examples were submitted by more than one person.

❖ "You're beautiful."

❖ "You add so much to this family."

❖ "You're really good at . . ."

❖ "I really like who you are."

❖ "How do you feel about that?" or "What do *you* think?"

❖ "I respect you."

❖ "You're more responsible than a lot of adults I know."

❖ "You're going to achieve whatever you want because of your great personality."

❖ "You did a wonderful job! I'm so proud of you."

❖ "I appreciate knowing I can count on you."

❖ "Your dad and I have loved you since the moment you were born, and we will never stop loving you."

❖ "You've got a good head on your shoulders."

❖ "You've got a tremendous amount of talent."

❖ "I believe in you."

❖ "You have a great sense of humor" or "You're fun to be with."

❖ "I really admire how you . . ."

❖ "Your hard work really shows."

❖ "I appreciate you."

❖ "I'm so lucky to know you."

Genuine appreciation comes without an agenda and with no attempt to change or control a child's behavior. Comments from important adults become a part of a child's belief system and self-perception, and can greatly influence the way a child grows.

8 Things to Remember About Saying "I Love You"

❖ Most important, remember to *say* it! Say it often! (None of this "I told you I loved you in 1994." This isn't like going to the dentist twice a year!)

❖ Remember that saying "I love you" is not the same as having loving feelings or doing loving things (like providing for your child, buying her things or washing her clothes). Kids need to experience love in many ways, including being told they are loved.

❖ Don't expect your kid to say "I love you, too." Tell her because you want to, because it's what you're feeling. Period.

❖ Avoid connecting it to something your child has done ("I love you when . . ."). Remember, "I love you" is a complete sentence. Keep it unconditional.

❖ If it's hard for you to say "I love you," write it down and leave the message under your kid's pillow. (One mother practiced saying it to the dog before she had the courage to say it out loud to her kids!)

❖ Following "I love you" with the word "but" is confusing and manipulative. Don't use "I love you" to "soften the blow" before identifying a problem that needs to be confronted or addressed. Just ask for the behavior you want (or want to stop).

❖ "I love you" is a private and personal exchange. Announcing these feelings to your kid in front of her friends can be embarrassing for everyone, especially at certain ages.

❖ Look in the mirror and say it to yourself (with no "but's" or qualifiers). Say it out loud. Say it until you can say it without laughing (or cringing). Mean it.

> *"The best advice I could give any parent would be to never pass up a chance to tell your kids that you love them. Touch them, cuddle and hug them often. Never part without saying 'I love you.'"*
>
> **—Andy Quiñones**
> parent

12 Ways to Increase Positivity in Your Interactions

❖ Distinguish between who your child is and what he does. Separate his behavior from his worth. (This makes it easier to love and accept him even when his behavior is neither lovable nor acceptable.)

❖ Focus on what your kid is doing right. Look for the positive and build on that.

❖ Recognize (and celebrate) achievements, accomplishments, effort and improvement.

❖ Attack the problem instead of the person. Asking for different behavior is more effective—and more positive—than accusations, name calling, put-downs or shaming. (For example, "The rest of these toys need to be picked up" rather than "You are so lazy!")

❖ Remind yourself to be positive. One parent framed an inspirational saying and hung it near the front door to greet him (and remind him) as soon as he came into the house. Another marked a bunch of index cards with plus signs and put them in places she'd see them so she could remember to be more positive.

❖ Create a reward-oriented home environment (rather than a punishment-oriented one).* Think of consequences as *positive* outcomes that are available when your child cooperates. Emphasize the good things that happen (or the good things your kid can do) when he follows through on his responsibilities.

❖ State your boundaries and contingencies as promises rather than threats. ("If you finish by noon . . ." rather than "If you don't . . .").

❖ Communicate what you want positively by changing "no" statements to "yes" statements: "Don't shout" becomes "Speak softly." "No! Don't color on that!" becomes "Wait! Here's some paper for you to color on. Please keep the crayons on the paper." Ask for the specific behaviors you want, rather than focusing on what you don't want.

❖ Rather than criticize your kid for suggesting or attempting a dumb idea, give him a choice of more positive options. Change responses like "Are you

---

* The word "reward" scares a lot of parents, probably because it suggests some kind of token or payment for doing things they want done. But "rewards" can also be things like having clean laundry when your kid remembers to put his clothes in the hamper, getting the car again as long as he comes home on time, or getting his favorite story read to him if he gets into pajamas with his teeth brushed by 7:00. Any positive outcome that is meaningful to your child can be a reward.

crazy? It's too cold to go outside in your T-shirt" to "It's cold outside. You can wear your sweatsuit outside, or you can wear your T-shirt in the house."

❖ To whatever extent is possible in your life, minimize your exposure to negative, toxic people, information and situations.

❖ Smile.

❖ Maintain your sense of humor.

15 Things to Remember About Reinforcing Positive Behavior

❖ Watch the tendency to focus on errors, mistakes, flaws and omissions. Deliberately look for what your child is doing right! (It's easier to recognize and reinforce positive behavior when you start noticing it.)

❖ Resist judging or connecting your child's worth to an accomplishment. Instead of saying "You're so good because you made the honor roll," try "All right! You made the honor roll! I know how hard you worked this semester." (Isn't she good and worthwhile even when she doesn't make the honor roll?)

❖ Use a two-step technique to recognize a behavior or accomplishment without reinforcing dependence, people-pleasing or the need for approval. *First, describe the behavior (without judging the behavior or the worth of your child):* "I see you got the car in on time," "Way to go! You got all your chores done," "You finished your homework." *Then tell how the positive behavior pays off for your child:* "You can borrow it again next weekend if you'd like," "Now you can watch TV (or go outside or use the phone)."

❖ Recognize positive behavior *after* it has occurred. Resist the temptation to flatter your child into cooperating by telling her how neat, smart or brave she is. (Once she acts neat, smart or brave, then acknowledge: "You organized your toys beautifully!" "You figured that out all by yourself!")

❖ Don't recognize someone else's behavior to try to motivate your child to do the same. "Your cousin Mabel writes her thank-you notes right away" or "Other kids your age aren't afraid of ghosts" will only reinforce resentment, inadequacy and competitiveness.

❖ Avoid using conditional approval as reinforcement. Comments like "I'm so happy when you do your chores" or "I love you when you get good grades" suggest that you wouldn't feel this way otherwise, that your happiness and love depend upon your child doing these things.

❖ Avoid presuming how your child feels, should feel or must feel as a result of the accomplishment ("You must be proud . . . ," "You should feel happy . . ."). The experience may have an entirely different meaning and value to her.

❖ Watch out for overkill! Children are naturally suspicious of "5-dollar reactions" to "10-cent events." Go ahead and celebrate a major breakthrough or achievement, but simple recognition and acknowledgment are probably enough for most day-to-day behaviors and accomplishments.

❖ If you give a compliment, do so without an agenda. If you tell your child that her hair looks pretty, don't load the statement with an expectation that she spend more time on her appearance, implying "See? Why can't you look this nice *all* the time?"

❖ If you want to tell your child she's wonderful, tell her. Just watch the tendency to connect her "wonderfulness" to something she has done. "You're such a neat kid." Period! Let your child know how and what you appreciate about her. Give your compliments freely—and frequently!

❖ Don't give a compliment as a way to introduce a complaint: "You played that piece beautifully. Too bad you're not doing so well in math." You may think you're saying something positive, but it's a sure bet your child will hear it as an attack.

❖ Stay in the present. Praising previous behavior ("But you *used* to be so neat!") is critical and manipulative.

❖ Some of the best reinforcement comes when your child experiences the positive outcomes of making good choices. Having access to the phone or TV at 7:30 because she finished her homework on time, going out to play because she cleaned up her room before her friends came over, or getting to eat dinner with the rest of the family because she got home on time are all positive consequences that reinforce your child's cooperative behavior.

❖ Reinforcers must be meaningful to a child. Saying "You picked up all your toys! Now you get to iron!" will probably discourage your child from ever picking up her toys again (unless, of course, she loves to iron). "Now you can play with them again tomorrow" or "Now I can tuck you in and read you your story" will probably be more effective (but only if playing with the toys tomorrow or hearing the story is more meaningful than not picking up the toys in the first place!).

❖ As behaviors become more internalized and automatic, they also self-reinforce. The need for *your* reinforcement diminishes. Acknowledge the positive anyhow—it's always nice to be appreciated!

PART IV

Skill Building, Learning and Personal Growth

Skill Building, Learning and Personal Growth

This section includes lists to help you build the skills and relationships that will help your child succeed in school and, certainly, later in life. You'll find ideas for improving your child's attitude toward learning, reading and homework, building good relationships with teachers, and encouraging the development of thinking skills, decision-making skills, creativity and the ability to follow directions.

You'll also encounter ways to build success and deal with mistakes and failures in positive ways. And you'll probably discover some great ways to have a lot of fun with your child in the process!

14 Ways to Encourage a Lifelong Love of Learning

❖ *Be* a lifelong learner. Become a student and a learning model. Take a class or try something new.

❖ Make learning a low-stress, fun experience. Avoid drills and pop quizzes. Encourage curiosity and exploration, with no expectations or pressure to perform.

❖ Look up words (together) if you don't know what they mean. When your child asks you questions, instead of just providing answers, say "Let's find out" and investigate together.

❖ Inspire a love of books. Read regularly. Let your child see you read. Read to your child, or let him read to you. *(See "31 Ways to Develop Literacy and a Love of Reading" for more information.)*

❖ Investigate things you're curious about and encourage your child to do the same.

❖ Never discourage a dream. Even though they're probably well intended, messages that suggest "Oh, you wouldn't like that" or "I don't think you'd be very good at that" are toxic and disabling.

❖ Encourage your child to try new things. Even if it turns out to be more difficult or less fun than he'd imagined, each new experience allows him to discover a little more about who he is and could be. (While there's value in sticking with something for a while, it's also valuable to recognize when it's time to move on to something else that may be a far better match.)

❖ Notice others who continue learning and trying new things. Point out models and examples of other life-long learners to your child.

❖ If your family watches TV, include at least some programming that is interesting, instructional and appropriate for the age and interests of your child. Talk about the shows you watch. Learn with your child!

❖ Respect your child's learning styles and preferences. (Some people really do learn better sitting on the floor than at a desk, listening to music, moving around, working with different levels of light or at different times of the day than you might.) Find out more about different ways people learn and the different learning preferences your child has.

❖ Tap into what you already love and see how your current interests connect with new things or take you in new directions. See how far you can stretch intellectually and creatively.

❖ Set a family goal to make a point of noticing or learning at least one thing you never saw or knew before. Model enthusiasm about learning something new every day. Make time daily for everyone to share what he or she learned.

❖ Help your child to develop basic learning and study skills, such as note taking, outlining, critical thinking, report preparation, test taking, organization and time management.

❖ Lifelong learners need to know how to learn and where to find things out! Teach your child to use and explore reference material to find out about things that interest him. In addition to enlisting traditional resources like the dictionary, thesaurus, encyclopedia or atlas, learning to use the library and online references can open up the world for your child—and you, too!

15 Ways to Accommodate Your Child's Success Needs

❖ Learn as much as you can about what's developmentally appropriate for children her age, what children typically can do or understand at that point in their lives.

❖ Be sure your child is developmentally capable of doing what you're asking and has the requisite skills to succeed. For example, does she have the motor development required to pour milk from a half-gallon container or the size, strength and information needed to safely operate a lawn mower or other piece of equipment or machinery?

❖ Make sure she has the necessary tools and equipment to do the job and that everything is working correctly.

❖ Pay attention to how she learns and remembers things. Does she need to touch or practice? Does she work best with an example, a picture or written directions? Can she remember verbal instructions and reminders? Be willing to explain things in different ways or ways that may be different from how you best understand.

❖ Anticipate, as best you can, all the possible ways your child might get or do something wrong, misunderstand, or be unsure about something. Don't assume she knows, even if she *should* know. Demonstrate what you want.

❖ Give her opportunities to practice new skills—and some time to get it right.

❖ Get her attention before you give her directions or important information. Make sure she's listening and not preoccupied or rushing out the door.

❖ Give simple, step-by-step directions. Be willing to explain things more than once without losing your patience or getting angry.

❖ Be very clear and specific. Words like *clean, good* or *early* probably have different meanings to you than they do to your child.

❖ Whenever possible, give instructions when you're feeling patient, especially if you're explaining something complicated or involved.

❖ Write down reminders or instructions. Many people remember things they see much better than things they hear. A note (or even a picture) taped to the refrigerator, bathroom mirror or TV may work much better than a dozen verbal reminders—and will be much more difficult for your child to "forget."

❖ Avoid offering options that are not actually available, even inadvertently. If you ask "Do you want to take a bath now?" you create an opportunity for conflict unless it's perfectly okay for her to say no. (If no is not an option, ask instead "Which of these toys would you like to play with in the tub?" "Which washcloth and towel do you want to use?" or "What would you like me to read to you while you're taking your bath?")

❖ Ask for feedback to establish clarity and commitment: "Tell me what you think I'm asking you to do," "Tell me your understanding of what I'm asking for," "Tell me how you're going to do (or remember) this."

❖ Ask your child to demonstrate or explain that she understands what you're asking her to do before asking or allowing her to do it on her own: "Show me how to put the CD back in the case" or "Pretend you're teaching me how to operate this stereo. What do I need to know?" (This works well when negotiating boundaries and limits, too: "Tell me what you just agreed to.")

❖ Teach your child to set goals, to translate her dreams into actions.

These suggestions will help you avoid unnecessary conflict and frustration likely to occur when your child doesn't understand what you want, when she's not clear on which options are available, or when she doesn't have the skills or developmental readiness to do what you're asking.

---

8 Things to Do When Your Child Makes a Mistake

❖ Help him see that mistakes are just opportunities to learn. Encourage him to try again.

❖ If he made the mistake because of a lack of understanding, explain or re-explain what he needs to know.

❖ Without yelling or criticizing, help him focus on what he's trying to accomplish: "How did you want these to look (or turn out)?" "What was supposed to happen?"

❖ Ask him what he might do differently next time. Let him predict or guess at the possible outcomes of a different approach.

❖ Trust in his ability to figure it out or find a solution. Help him rethink his approach, strategy or goal, but fight the temptation to fix it for him.

❖ Avoid expressing disapproval or disappointment. Instead, try "Oops!" "That's interesting!" or "That wasn't what you had in mind, was it?"

❖ Describe the situation without blaming: "Too many sweets can cause a tummy ache" is different from "You're sick because you overate."

❖ Don't yell, shame or call him "stupid." There's a difference between *making* a mistake and *being* one.

13 Ways to Build Decision-Making Skills

❖ Look for opportunities to offer choices, even though it will often seem easier or more expedient to simply issue a command.

❖ Let your child decide how she's going to solve a problem, even though it will often be easier to simply tell her what to do.

❖ Ask your child for her input about food, letting her choose which juice or dessert she wants, what she wants for a snack (or meal, if convenient) or whether she wants a second helping, for example. When she is able, encourage her to plan an entire meal.

❖ Give her opportunities to make decisions about her clothes, from deciding between two sweaters, for example, to being completely responsible for how she dresses (and wears her hair).

❖ Give her a TV "allowance" of a certain number of hours per week. Allow her to determine how she'll "spend" the number of hours she has on the shows or channels available to her.

❖ Let her determine how she wants to arrange or decorate her room (or some space of her own).

❖ Let her decide whether she needs more practice on a certain task or skill before moving on to something harder.

❖ Let her decide which of two things she wants to do first, or select two out of three chores that need to be done.

❖ Allow her to offer concrete evidence to show that she is ready to handle a new privilege or responsibility.

❖ Allow her to be in charge of managing certain aspects of her life—to decide, for example, how she plans to keep track of her favorite toys, find things she needs in her dresser, or remember everything she'll need for school the next day.

❖ When she has a problem, help her identify possible strategies or solutions and explore what might happen if she makes certain choices.

❖ Request that your child take some responsibility for resolving a conflict in a way that will work for everyone involved: "Tell me how you're going to make sure that I get all my phone messages when

I'm not home." (One mother insisted that her son write out all the details before allowing his telephone privileges to continue.)

❖ Give her space to make poor (but not life-threatening) decisions. Sometimes the best way to learn good decision-making skills is to make bad decisions!

19 Ways to Build Thinking Skills

❖ Ask open-ended questions: "What went well for you in school today?" or "What did you like best about today?" instead of yes-or-no questions like "Did you have a nice day?" or "Was your dance class fun?"

❖ Talk about TV shows or movies you've seen, books you've read, or places you've visited (or heard about) that may interest him. Enlarge his world by helping him see beyond the scope of his own experiences.

❖ When your child proposes solutions to problems, ask him questions like "What might happen next if you do that?" "How do you think you'll feel?" "Will that cause a problem for anyone else?" or "What else can you do if that doesn't work?"

❖ Use mistakes or seemingly poor choices as opportunities to help your kid rethink goals and strategies: "How do you think you could have avoided what happened?" or "What do you think you'll do differently next time?"

❖ Talk about common expressions like "It's raining cats and dogs." Ask questions like "What would it be like if that really happened?" "How do you think that expression got started?" "How else could we describe the rain?"

❖ Buy games, books, activity books or toys that require thinking or problem solving.

❖ Use concrete objects to help with concept and vocabulary development. For example, play with your kid using a collection of things like buttons or match packs.* Ask him to find his favorite and tell you why he likes it, or to find one that's similar and tell you how they're alike. Ask questions like "What kind of clothing do you think this button came from?" or "Which matches came from a different state?" Encourage him to start his own collections.

❖ Place an object in a pillowcase—a toy car, a small pumpkin, a kitchen item or utensil, a shoe, a string of beads, or a stuffed animal, for example.** Ask your child to guess what's in the bag, either by feeling it through the pillowcase or by reaching in and touching

---

* Teach match safety or remove the matches first.

** Nothing sharp or dangerous, please. Also, nothing alive (or, for that matter, dead).

it with his eyes closed. Ask for different possibilities—don't require that he get it "right."

❖ Provide a variety of plastic cups, bowls and containers in different shapes and sizes for your kid to play with in a sandbox or at the beach, in a sink half-full of water, or in a large basin filled with uncooked rice.

❖ Fill a play area or toy box with objects that represent a variety of shapes, colors and textures to provide visual and tactile (touch) stimulation. You might include things like kitchen counter sample tiles, a book of wallpaper samples or different kinds of fabrics. Also, make sure you have lots of books, magazines and fun catalogs on hand.

❖ Save or collect old or broken clocks, telephones, radios or toys for your child to take apart.

❖ Make sure his toy collection includes at least one set of materials for building or constructing, like Lego or K'nex.

❖ Let him make something from plans—for example, putting together a model or a puzzle, laying out a garden, making a book bag or vest from a pattern, constructing a woodworking project, following a recipe. (Make sure the project is appropriate for your kid's age, interests and abilities.) Help as necessary.

❖ Help him learn to use home, library, video and Internet resources to get information he needs.

❖ Go through your own thinking process aloud, weighing positives and negatives. Ask your child for input when you're solving a problem. Encourage him to solve problems the same way.

❖ Ask thought-provoking questions like "What would be good about living forever? What would be bad?" or "If you could only have one superpower, which one would you choose? Why?" (Try this while you're stuck in traffic with your kid, waiting for someone, or standing in line.)

❖ Ask your child for his perspective or opinion about something in the news, something that happened to a friend, or what he's learning in school, for example. Respect his thoughts and ideas, even ones that seem outrageous or shocking to you. (If he's trying to get a reaction and all you say is "H'mm. That's interesting," he might revert to less dramatic commentary.)

❖ Discuss experiences you and your kid have shared. Ask for his impressions and recollections. (Be aware that some people notice and remember details, while others get more general images or feelings when looking at the same things.)

❖ Add to the amount of responsibility your kid has as he increasingly demonstrates an ability to anticipate, plan and make decisions on his own.

23 Ways to Encourage
Creativity and Imagination

❖ Give your child time and space to be creative. Make sure she has some unstructured time in her life. Balance her responsibilities (homework, chores, after-school lessons and activities) with freedom to play and fantasize. Make it okay to spend some time doing absolutely nothing.

❖ Make it okay for your child to be silly and frivolous.

❖ Be silly and frivolous *yourself.* Try new things. Play. Be spontaneous. Acknowledge and appreciate your own creativity.

❖ Get her a journal. Respect her right to keep her writings or drawings private.

❖ Ask "what if" questions.

❖ Ask for alternate endings to stories. Take turns writing or telling parts of a story.

❖ Make and do things together.

* Indulge your child's curiosity whenever possible. Provide information, resources, instruction and materials to help her explore new areas of interest.

* Respect her right to move on if she discovers that something she was curious about is less interesting or fulfilling than she anticipated. Leave the door open for her to try again later.

* Let go of expectations and attachments. Focus on the journey, the process of exploring, discovering and creating—not the final products and the accolades you'd like to see her receive, or the pride you'll take in her accomplishments.

* Make mud pies or sand castles.

* Find a large box for her to use as a playhouse, a spaceship or a time machine, for example.

* Let her color outside the lines. Make it okay to do something wrong, do it differently or even make mistakes. Fight the urge to fix it, do it over or make it right.

* Make it okay to not be good at something.

* Respect "oddball" ideas. Don't stifle or discourage your child, unless trying something would be

physically harmful to her or others. Resist the urge to warn her that "that won't work." Let her explore and find out for herself.

❖ Save your old clothes or hit garage sales to build a "costume wardrobe" for your child to wear.

❖ Let her turn the couch cushions into a fort.

❖ Get your child a camera and some film. Show her the basics and talk to her a bit about composition and lighting. Then turn her loose!

❖ At dinner or before bed, take turns describing imaginary things: "I'm thinking about an elephant driving a bus" or "I can picture little birdhouses growing all over our apple tree." (This is *not* just for little kids!)

❖ Honor her imaginary friends.

❖ When you're waiting in line with your child, pick out other people in the room (or store) and make up a story about them: "That woman is a superhero in disguise. When she's not shopping for shoes, she . . . ," "That man is searching for his true love, who was turned into a grocery clerk by an evil wizard after. . . ." Ask your child to finish the story or add to it as you take turns. Be outrageous!

- ❖ Create a space where it's okay to make messy projects (for example, with paint, glue, glitter, clay or mud).

- ❖ Lose the perfectionism. Criticism is deadly.

10 Ways to Encourage an Appreciation for the Arts

❖ Occasionally, play music in the house (or car) that's different from the music you usually play.

❖ Have family sing-alongs.

❖ Read poetry to your child. Encourage him to write his own poems (and bind them in a book when you have a variety—either from that particular child or from everyone in the family).

❖ Watch concerts, plays and art-related programs on TV.

❖ Walk through a gallery or display and ask "What if you lived in that garden?" "What if the crazy shapes in that painting were a playground?" or "What if you could be friends with the little girl in the painting?" Chat about the possibilities.

❖ Play a famous classical piece on the stereo and "act it out." For example, if it's a dark, foreboding sound, creep around on all fours, pretending to be alligators. If it's light and airy, dance about like fairies or fly like birds.

❖ Watch for local presentations of programs, exhibits, plays or concerts you can enjoy together.

❖ Encourage your child to explore different types of cultural events. If you've never been to a ballet or a bluegrass concert, for example, look for an opportunity to attend one together (or watch it on video). Talk about how this experience compares with what you normally watch or listen to. Respect different preferences and reactions to new experiences, and remember that some tastes are acquired with age and time!

❖ Give your child opportunities to study or participate in art-related activities that interest him. Look to the schools or community college, your place of worship, the YMCA, your local department of parks and recreation, a community center, or organizations like the Boy Scouts or Girl Scouts for classes, clubs, or private instruction in painting and other crafts, music (instruments or singing) or drama.

❖ Encourage your child to work with different crafts or media. Create a space for him to make his own art. Display his masterpieces.

31 Ways to Develop Literacy and a Love of Reading

❖ Keep a wide variety of reading material on hand, including different types of books—"easy" books, picture books, reference books, comic books—catalogs and magazines.

❖ Read to your child (even if she's old enough to read to herself). Snuggle up and make books feel good.

❖ When you read to your child, read for periods of time that are comfortable for both of you. Build "listening stamina" if necessary.

❖ Be enthusiastic and lively when you read to your child, even if you're reading the same book for the hundredth time!

❖ Read, read, read! Model a love of reading.

❖ Make time to read—*just* for reading! Help your child do the same.

❖ Let your child read to you or to other children.

❖ Make chore charts with pictures or words.

❖ Have a party and invite children to come as their favorite storybook characters.

❖ Get your child a library card.

❖ Respect personal preferences. Allow your child to make choices about the books she wants to read (or have you read to her). Resist making judgments about her selections because her interests are different from yours, or when she chooses a book you think is too "young" for her.*

❖ Take your child to readings or storytelling sessions at your library, place of worship, bookstores, or community center. Take her to book signings to meet her favorite authors.

❖ Encourage your child to participate in read-a-thons.

❖ Help with school book fairs.

❖ Encourage your child to keep a private journal or diary (which no one else can read unless invited).

❖ Encourage your child to write her own books or stories. Bind her stories and illustrations, or keep them

---

* Common-sense considerations apply for topics that may be too scary or otherwise inappropriate for individual children at particular ages. However, books with serious, even controversial messages or seemingly "offensive" points of view can be especially valuable as discussion starters or ways to explore personal and family values.

in a notebook. (Many print or copy shops can laminate covers and provide different types of bindings.)

❖ Point out letters and words on signs, buildings or packages. Ask your child to look for certain letters, words, shapes or colors when you're in the car together or in the supermarket.

❖ Explain vocabulary as you read, rather than asking your child to look it up.

❖ Read a book together and then watch it on video or go to a children's theater production. (Or read the book after you see the play or video.)

❖ Get books on tape for your child to listen to. Story tapes can entertain some children for fairly long stretches of time and can be particularly useful on long drives or in the supermarket, for example.

❖ Be willing to abandon a book in the middle if your child doesn't like it.

❖ Have each person in your family read the same book and then talk about it.

❖ Have your child write letters to her favorite authors. (If she's too young to write, have her dictate her letters to you for you to write.) You can send letters to authors in care of their publishers.

❖ Encourage your child to tell stories to go with pictures or music, to make up a song to go with a certain story, to illustrate a story you read to her (or one she listens to on tape), or to act out a story after you've read it together.

❖ Label things in the house, especially in her room.

❖ Give books as gifts. Ask for books as gifts for yourself.

❖ Let the books you read inspire fun follow-up activities. Look for more information about a particular place, event, topic, holiday or animal, for example, that you read about. Build, cook or make something that was mentioned or described in the book.

❖ Talk about the characters in your child's favorite books as if they were a part of your life (for example, as if they were in the car with you, going to school with your child or having dinner with your family).

❖ Ask your child to imagine herself in situations she reads about, to describe how she would dress, feel or react in those situations.

❖ Let your child respond emotionally to stories she's read.

❖ Turn off the television from time to time. Restrict the number of hours your family watches TV.

9 Ways to Minimize Problems
with Homework

❖ Discuss and agree to specific times for doing homework. Many kids need a bit of a break between school and homework time, although some will want to come home and "get it out of the way" while they still have a little momentum.

❖ Discuss and agree to a specific place for doing homework, preferably somewhere away from distractions that would interrupt your child's concentration.

❖ Make homework *his* responsibility. Let him do the work on his own. Help as needed, or look things over when he's done if you want, but watch the temptation (or the belief that you need) to sit with him while he's doing the work.

❖ Make sure he has the materials he needs to carry homework assignments to and from school (a book bag, backpack or loose-leaf binder), and a date book or notebook to keep track of assignment details and due dates.

❖ Show an interest in his work. Ask him to explain his assignments to you, which one he's going to do first, how he plans to do a particular assignment. Let him tell you which teachers give the most homework, which assignments are most interesting, what kind of credit he gets for doing assignments, what happens if his work is late or incorrect.

❖ Respect his learning style preferences. Some kids work and learn better when sitting on the floor, working with the radio on, working with a friend or working in brighter (or dimmer) light than you might prefer yourself. Give him a chance to self-manage and find out what works best for him.

❖ Remember that some kids need breaks after a specific amount of time or when the work is completed. Help him select break activities and time intervals that won't slow him down or make it hard for him to get back to work.

❖ Allow certain privileges only when homework is done. (You may need to specify what "done" means. One parent explained that "done" meant complete and legible, while another specified a certain level of accuracy in the work.)

❖ As a part of his homework routine, encourage your kid to take a few minutes to make sure his "school stuff" is neat and organized, either before he gets started on his assignments, right after he finishes (to get everything ready for the next morning), or both.

17 Ways to Build Positive Relationships with Your Child's Teachers

❖ Make initial contacts early in the year, during a non-conflict time. Don't wait for a problem to arise.

❖ At the beginning of the year, ask your child's teachers about their goals, expectations, rules and limits. Find out how often, and under what circumstances, you can expect to hear from them.

❖ Become an active participant at the school or in school organizations. Join the PTA, for example, or offer to volunteer in the classroom.

❖ Make sure the school has information about your schedule and availability.

❖ Focus on the positive. When you're so moved, send your child's teachers "good notes" about good things you've heard about them (from your child or others), what you appreciate or what they're doing great!

❖ If a teacher calls to discuss a problem, ask for specifics: "What is she doing?" "When did this start?" "How often does this happen?" "What are your consequences for this type of behavior?" If necessary, ask the teacher to refrain from making judgments about your child's personality or character, and stick to the behavior.

* Listen.

* Avoid speaking for your child, even if she's very young. Contribute your observations, needs or personal experiences and encourage your child to express her own.

* Avoid automatically taking the teacher's side. Also, resist defending or making excuses for your child. Fight the urge to rescue her from the negative outcomes of poor choices she makes. Do your best to stay out of the middle of the problem.

* Avoid taking responsibility for solving problems between your child and her teacher. It's not unreasonable to expect the school to have its own consequences for the rules it establishes. You can still support the teacher without punishing or correcting your child for an infraction you did not witness.

* Don't ask a teacher to punish or withhold privileges from your child for infractions that occurred at home.

* Avoid approaching a teacher reactively. Keep the focus on how you can all get what you want.

❖ Avoid becoming defensive or feeling the need to prove your competence as a parent. Resist the temptation to punish your child to compensate for the feeling that she "made you look bad" in front of someone else.*

❖ If either you or the teacher starts to become angry, reactive, defensive or hostile, request a short break for everyone to regroup, calm down and refocus. If necessary, consider mediation (a neutral third party) to help keep the focus on the child's best interests and opportunities for success.

❖ Keep track of contacts with the school, positive and negative. Note the date, the issue discussed, strategies proposed, and a time and way to follow up. Check in at a later time, if appropriate, to see how things are going.

❖ If you ask for feedback from the teacher, be reasonable in your requests. Teachers have more than enough to do (and lots of other students to deal with). Strive to find a routine or system that works for you all.

---

* Feeling embarrassed or shamed by your child's behavior has little to do with your child. If you frequently find yourself having a hard time separating how your child acts from your sense of adequacy as a parent, you're probably experiencing a lot more stress in your relationship than is necessary, simply from your efforts to control your child in order to feel okay about yourself. Separating yourself (and your worth) from your child's behavior can be an enormous challenge and may be easier to accomplish with some kind of support or help.

❖ Help your child resolve conflicts with teachers on her own. Remember, she will have to deal with different individuals throughout her life, when you may not be around to advise her or bail her out. Help her develop the flexibility to succeed in a variety of relationships. *(See "18 Questions You Can Ask When Your Child Says 'My Teacher Hates Me'" for more ideas.)*

18 Questions You Can Ask When Your Child Says "My Teacher Hates Me"

❖ "What happened?"

❖ "What bothers you the most about this situation?"

❖ "What exactly do you want?" (Or "If you had a magic wand, how would you make this turn out?")

❖ "How can you get what you want without creating additional problems for yourself (or anyone else)?"

❖ "What have you tried that's worked with this person?" (Or "What's worked for you in the past?" "What works with your other teachers?" or "What seems to work for the other kids?")

❖ "What else could you try?"

❖ "What are you risking by doing that?" (Or "What are you risking by making that choice?")

❖ "What kind of backup plans do you have if that doesn't work out?"

❖ "How do you think she'll feel about that?"

❖ "How do you think you'll feel later (or afterward)?"

❖ "If you were the other person, what would you want from you?" (Or "What do you think the other person wants?")

❖ "What would you have to do differently to make this work the way you want it to?"

❖ "If the situation doesn't change, what can you do to handle it better?"

❖ "How important is it for you to pass this class?"

❖ "What are you willing to do to pass this class?"

❖ "What will happen if you don't pass this class?"

❖ "Can you live with that?" (Or "Is it worth it?")

❖ "What are you willing to change to get what you want?"

Your child will encounter difficult people throughout his life. There will be times when you'll want to intervene, but watch the temptation to smooth out problems your child has with others. In the long run, it's probably far more helpful to teach him to find better ways to take care of himself in challenging situations and relationships. By asking these questions, or questions like these, you help your child take responsibility for finding solutions by exploring the dimensions of the problem, the options he has available and the outcomes of possible choices he can make. (Don't forget to listen!)

(See "6 Reasons Not to Give Your Child Advice" and "9 Benefits of Asking Questions Instead of Giving Answers" for more information.)

PART V

Problem
Solving and
Prevention

Problem Solving and Prevention

Here's where we get into specifics—ways to minimize or prevent problems that can occur in particular situations. In addition to exploring issues related to bedtime, food, health and safety, car trips, chores or money, you'll find a few more general lists to help your children build independent problem-solving skills.

I understand the desire to jump right to these pages, to find ways to solve or respond to specific problems. A word of caution here: Very often, problems in a particular area are symptoms of larger problems or power struggles in the relationship. If you haven't looked over the lists in the previous sections, you may have a hard time placing this information in the context of creating a win-win, solutions-oriented relationship with your child. Keep in mind that all of these lists work together toward that end. Change your approach to monsters in the closet, and you change a piece of the relationship. Although it probably doesn't matter where you jump into the loop, try to keep the big picture in mind—the relationship itself.

6 Reasons *Not* to Give
Your Child Advice

❖ Giving advice robs your child of the opportunity to think of possible solutions herself.

❖ It interferes with her ability to develop confidence and competence in problem solving.

❖ It prevents her from taking responsibility for her problems and teaches her to depend on someone else for solving her problems.

❖ It conveys a lack of trust in her ability to solve problems on her own.

❖ Your advice could be wrong and could actually create additional problems for your kid.

❖ Giving advice allows your child to blame *you* if your advice doesn't work out.

Resisting the impulse to give advice can be an enormous challenge. This ability requires time, patience and a willingness to suspend your agenda (wanting your child to solve a problem in a particular way). Rather than telling or advising, *ask questions.* Your questions and guidance help her take responsibility for the problem and its solution, a skill that will come in handy when you're not there to tell her what to do. *(See "9 Benefits of Asking Questions Instead of Giving Answers" for more information.)*

"Remember, advice is often free, and too often,
we get what we pay for."

—**Bob Algozzine**
author, *Teacher's Little Book of Wisdom*

9 Benefits of Asking Questions
Instead of Giving Answers*

❖ Questions help your child explore dimensions of a problem.

❖ Questions help your child explore his available options.

❖ Questions help your child identify his goals and intentions.

❖ Questions draw solutions from your child.

❖ Questions communicate your trust in your child's ability to solve a problem.

❖ Questions place the responsibility for finding a solution on your child.

❖ Questions allow you to help your child anticipate probable outcomes of various choices, helping him evaluate the choices he has.

---

* This does not mean using questions to disguise criticism or advice. "What can you do to solve this problem?" is very different from "How could you be so stupid?" or "Why don't you just tell her how you feel?"

❖ Questions build confidence and independence in problem solving.

❖ The process of asking instead of telling puts you in the role of facilitator or guide rather than rescuer. It helps build skills and confidence your child can rely on when an adult isn't around to tell him what to do.

Imagine the learning your child can experience when you ask questions like "How would you like your friend to treat you?" "What have you already tried?" "What else can you do?" "What might happen if you do that?" "How will you feel if that happens?" or "What else can you do?" Compare this process with what he learns when you simply say "Well, just ignore her" or "Go play with somebody else." Even though a solution may be quite evident to you, there is great value in your child's exploring the problem and possible solutions with you as his guide!

11 Ways to Encourage Cooperation with Chores

❖ Start young. Even preschoolers can help dust, pick things up or put things away. One mother had her three-year-old help her match socks and fold pillow-cases on laundry day, while others received help with tasks like unloading specific items from the dish-washer, sorting laundry or making the bed.

❖ Make chores and household responsibilities a priority. Make sure that the "fun stuff" (the things your child would rather be doing) is available *after* chores are done.

❖ Break down large chores into manageable units. "Clean the kitchen" can be overwhelming, but "Clear off the counters," "Empty the dishwasher (or dish drainer)," "Wipe the table" or "Sweep the floor" is much less daunting.

❖ Create a "chore chart" or checklist for your child to mark after she completes each task. Use drawings or pictures for prereaders. Make sure you include fun and easy tasks on the chore charts, things she ordinarily does (or doesn't mind doing) to create a sense of accomplishment and give her easy things to check off!

❖ Offer choices about chores. For example, ask which of two chores she wants to do first, or which chore she plans to do today. You can even ask her to commit to a chore or a number of chores from a list, provided her selections are age- and ability-appropriate.

❖ Before simply assigning chores, ask for some input about which chores she prefers doing. Whenever possible, accommodate her preferences.

❖ If she's really resistant to a particular chore, offer to trade her one of your chores that you really dislike doing, or "gang up" on the chores you both dislike, doing them together to get them out of the way.

❖ Make sure she has the necessary instruction and materials for completing her chores successfully.

❖ Make sure there are adequate (and, if possible, clearly labeled) places to put things away, and that your child can reach the shelves, hooks, storage boxes, milk crates and other needed supplies in order to complete her chores.

❖ Have an incentive—preferably some family activity— for finishing chores by a certain time.

❖ Offer a "bonus" such as not having to do chores—
or certain chores—for a day if she does her chores
without being reminded, if she finishes before the
deadline or if she does her chores a specified number
of days or weeks in a row. (One mother gave her son
a list of 10 things he needed to do to clean his room
each week and offered to do "the two most yucky
jobs" for him if he got the other eight done by a
certain day and time.)

3 Ways to Deal with a
Messy Room*

❖ Show your child how to make his bed, run the vacuum cleaner, and put away toys and clothing. Make sure he has enough drawers, hooks and storage bins. (Labeling may help.) After that, leave it up to him.

❖ If he complains that he can't find things or that he keeps tripping on his way to the bathroom at night, sympathize: "Yeah, that's a drag" or "Oh, I hate when that happens." Resist the temptation to yell, blame him for his troubles or be sarcastic—and definitely resist the urge to go in and clean up for him! Ask him what he's going to do to solve this problem. Hold him responsible for the state of his belongings and the consequences of letting things get out of hand.

❖ Close the door. Really.

---

* This refers to a child's own room, not one shared by the rest of the family. If your child shares a room with a sibling who is a lot neater or messier, help them find ways to work things out themselves.

7 Choices You Can Offer at Bath Time

❖ "Which toys would you like to take in the tub?"*

❖ "Which washcloth (or towel) would you like to use?"

❖ "Which story would you like me to read to you while you're in the tub (or after your bath)?"

❖ "Which bathroom would you like to use?" (If more than one is available.)

❖ "Would you rather take a bath or a shower?" (If age-appropriate.)

❖ "Which show or videotape do you want to watch afterward (if your bath is finished in time)?"

❖ "Which soap or shampoo do you prefer?"

Most of the time, taking a bath will not be negotiable. However, choices like these give your child some control over the event and will often eliminate power struggles or resistance.

---

* You may want to specify how many toys she can choose. Make sure the selection of available toys is appropriate for bath time.

12 Ways to Avoid Problems at Bedtime

❖ Establish a routine and stick to it. Bedtime rituals might include a snack, bathing, brushing teeth, putting on pajamas, reading, saying prayers, snuggling and cuddling, and talking about the day or making plans for tomorrow.

❖ Discuss routines, limits and any changes beforehand so your child will know what to expect.

❖ Offer choices and accommodate preferences when you can. Letting your child decide which washcloth to use in the tub, which story she wants you to read to her or which pajamas she wants to wear invites greater involvement and control, which can ultimately lead to more cooperative behavior.

❖ Keep it simple. If your kid is not used to a regular set of bedtime behaviors, start with one or two rituals and gradually increase the complexity of the routine.

❖ Be prepared to change routines as your child gets older and more independent.

❖ Start early enough to allow time for the entire routine.

❖ Keep bedtime (and the time to start getting ready for bed) the same, except for rare and special occasions.

❖ Determine who sleeps where and stick to it.

❖ Respect nighttime fears and do what you can to help your kid feel safe. *(See "14 Ways to Help Your Child Deal with Monsters in the Closet" for more information.)*

❖ Participate in some of the bedtime routines, even if only coming in to tuck your child in and kiss her goodnight. Bedtime can be a terrific time for sharing and interacting.

❖ Reserve quiet activities for evening. Many children have a hard time settling down and falling asleep after rough or vigorous play.

❖ Increase your child's responsibility for her own bedtime. Many parents have great success allowing their children to determine their own bedtime (as long as the kids stay in their own rooms after a certain time) and find that their kids quickly figure out how much sleep they need when they have to get up to an alarm the next day.

14 Ways to Help Your Child Deal with Monsters in the Closet

❖ Hang a "monster deflector" in your child's room or over his bed. You can use a small mirror, dream catcher, mobile, picture of an angel, red ribbon or religious icon, for example, to keep monsters away.

❖ As a part of the bedtime routine, you or your child can use a broom to sweep the monsters out of the closet and into the garage or basement, or out the door until the monsters quit coming back.

❖ Let your child sleep in monster-proof pajamas (or T-shirts or socks).

❖ Turn the pillow over to the non-monster side. (This also works after a nightmare.)

❖ Make or buy some "monster spray" or "monster repellent." (One parent used an old spray bottle from a window-cleaning product, washed it out, filled it with water and wrote "Monster Spray" on a blank label, which she put on the bottle.)

❖ Leave a light on in your child's room. (Or get a night-light—preferably one that doesn't throw scary shadows on the wall!)

❖ Give him a stuffed animal to watch over him (and for him to watch over).

❖ Play soft, soothing music or a tape of "white noise" to mask scary sounds as he's falling asleep.

❖ Put a chair in front of the closet door.

❖ Encourage him to pick up his clothes and put them away so there are no scary-looking lumps on the dresser, chair, doorknob or floor.

❖ Let your dog sleep in your child's room.

❖ Give your child a flashlight (especially helpful when he has to go to the bathroom in the dark).

❖ "Zap" the monster with a beam of light from a flashlight to make it go away.

❖ Announce, in a loud voice, that it's late and time for the monsters to go home to their own houses *right now!* (Their mommies and daddies are looking for them.)

Telling your child that there's no such thing as monsters is not as reassuring as taking action to help him feel safe. Ridiculing his fears or being impatient with him will probably only make things worse. (Most parents report that monsters tend to quit being a problem when their children don't have to invest much in defending their reality.) In the meantime, reassure him that he is safe, that monsters are only "real" in our imaginations or on TV, and that you will be nearby to protect and take care of him.

10 Things to Remember About Potty Training Your Child

❖ Don't push. Signs of interest and readiness might include curiosity and awareness, a desire to wear underpants instead of diapers, or the ability to let you know when she has to go. Once you start, be prepared to back off for a while, if necessary, and try again later (in a few days or weeks).

❖ Don't be too demanding. Understand that this process involves good days, bad days, "remembering" too late, forgetting altogether and unexpected backsliding after terrific progress.

❖ Major changes in the child's life can trigger a regression—a new baby or a different preschool, for example. Give your child some time to adjust.

❖ Make "sitting on the potty" (regular or training) a part of your evening ritual, a place to sit and relax while you talk or read to your child—whether she goes or not. (One mother said this was most effective if she ran water while she read.)

❖ Dress your child in clothing that is easy to get in and out of. Zippers, snaps, buckles, jumpsuits or overalls can sabotage even the most alert and dedicated child.

❖ Make hand washing a part of the routine for both of you.

❖ Focus on the positives. Be enthusiastic about your child's successes. Negative responses (calling your child a baby, comparing her with a toilet-trained friend, scolding, scowling or looking disgusted) can seriously impede a child's progress.

❖ Never hit, shame or punish a child for a relapse. This isn't a moral issue or even a personal failure for you or your child. Clean it up (or, if she's old enough, have her clean herself up) and go on.

❖ Resist pressure from family and friends. Your child is right on schedule.

❖ Remember you are training a child who will grow best with your love and patience. Keep the big picture in mind. You won't be working on this skill forever. Honest.

16 Ways to Avoid Conflicts over Food

❖ Ask your child for his input. Let him plan the menu for a particular meal, decide which vegetable he'd like, or tell what he'd like for dessert (perhaps selecting from the two or three options you suggest).

❖ Identify a particular day each month (or each week) for "kid's choice." Let your child choose the meal, main dish or the restaurant for a family dinner. If you have more than one child, your children can take turns each week or choose as a group.

❖ Respect your child's preferences. Look for alternate ways to meet specific nutritional needs. Prepare less-favorite foods in different ways.

❖ Serve smaller portions and make seconds an option.

❖ Let your child serve himself, especially if he's resistant to eating or in the habit of fighting with you over food.

❖ Don't try to force your child to eat foods he dislikes or to eat when he says he's full or not hungry.

❖ If your child *hates* what you've fixed, have an easy-fix alternative available, like cereal, crackers and cheese, or peanut butter and jelly. Encourage your child to get or fix these alternatives himself as soon as he's old enough to do so.

❖ Eliminate power struggles with a child who is reluctant to come to the table, especially if he has come to depend on you calling him a number of times, getting angry and then carrying him to the table. Let him know when the family is going to eat in terms he can understand ("when this TV show is over," "when the timer in the kitchen goes off") and that after a certain time, "the kitchen is closed." At the specified time, proceed normally, whether he comes or not. After the meal or after a reasonable time, clear the table. If he doesn't make it on time, encourage him for next time: "We'll have a great breakfast in the morning."*

❖ Encourage your child to help with the shopping, planning, preparation or serving.

---

* Try this approach *only* if you are bothered by the power struggle, if you mind having to call your child to the table over and over, or if you mind serving your family in "shifts." Yes, you will feel horrible. You might not even be able to eat yourself. But of the parents who had the courage to follow through on this strategy, not one reported having to do it twice. (A few parents allowed a piece of fruit or some juice for a child who had "missed" a meal.)

❖ Avoid using food as either a reward or punishment. Especially watch the urge to use sweets as motivators or rewards.

❖ Resist the temptation to use food (especially sweets) to cheer up your child when he's down, or to use food as a pacifier when your child is lonely, distressed or overly excited.

❖ Teach your child to say "No, thank you" (instead of "yeeeech") when offered foods he doesn't like (and to firmly and politely resist when offered foods he is allergic to or can't tolerate).

❖ If your child says "No, thank you" to you, respect his wishes (as you would an adult's). Don't pressure him to eat something he doesn't want by talking about how much time you spent preparing it, how happy it would make you if he'd eat it, or how other children are starving.

❖ Prepare your child's favorite meals once in a while.

❖ Try to make mealtimes as relaxed and stress-free as possible. This is not a good time to criticize, lecture, or bring up highly charged issues or conflicts. Do not make the dinner table a battleground.

❖ Remember that tastes change. Most children get more courageous about trying new things, develop new tastes and outgrow many of their early dislikes. Be patient.

Children typically have fewer problems with food ("picky eating," undereating or overeating) in an environment in which parents are neither pushing them to maintain a certain appearance or weight, nor trying to control what they eat. Encouragement, acceptance, empowerment and trusting a child's ability to self-regulate his intake can go a long way in preventing "food fights" and eating problems.

"Children must be in the driver's seat when it comes to their bodies and their eating."

—**Jane R. Hirschmann, C.S.W., and
Lela Zaphiropoulos, C.S.W.**
psychotherapists, authors of
Preventing Childhood Eating Problems

10 Ways to Minimize or Avoid Problems at the Grocery Store

❖ If possible, go early in the day when the stores are less crowded and your child is well rested.

❖ Tell your child exactly what she can get *before* you go. Be specific (one candy bar, two videos, her own box of cereal or a toy under five dollars, for example). Stick to the plan.

❖ If you're not prepared to buy your child anything, let her know ahead of time.

❖ Go in organized. Keep shopping trips with your child as short as possible.

❖ Ask for her input or let her decide between two or three types of cookies, cereals, fruit, desserts, juice, snacks or frozen dinners, for example.

❖ If she's old enough, let her help you find things in the store by herself and bring them to you. (One mother used labels or pictures on coupons to help her children find certain things in particular aisles.)

❖ If your child has to stay in the shopping cart, bring
  a few things for her to do or listen to while you're
  shopping.

❖ If the store has kid-size shopping carts, let your child
  have one for the things she picks out (or for things
  you pick out together, or the things you select that she
  likes or wants.)

❖ As she gets older, involve her more in the planning,
  budgeting and selecting. Eventually, consider allowing her to do the shopping herself.

❖ If shopping is really a problem, find a buddy to watch
  your child while you shop. Bring back a little thank-
  you gift for this person and agree to a time when you
  will watch your buddy's child when he or she goes to
  the store.

11 Ways to Avoid Problems over Money or Buying

❖ Let your child know what you're willing to buy him or how much he can have to spend *before* you go to the store.

❖ If you don't plan to buy your child a particular item he wants, let him know beforehand. (One parent invited her son to browse the toy section of his favorite store and asked him to tell her three things he *wished* he could have. She promised to keep his preferences in mind when it was time to buy.)

❖ If your child can't have what he wants, redirect his attention to something he *can* have: "We're not buying any candy on this trip. You can pick out the kind of cereal you'd like."

❖ Before you give your child an allowance, be clear about all aspects of your arrangement. Talk with your child about expenses he'll be expected to pay for himself, any restrictions on the use of the allowance, requirements for receiving or earning the allowance, what portion of the allowance must be saved, availability of advances (and arrangements for repaying), or ways to earn extra money when he needs it. You might even want to write out a "contract," but with or without this backup, stick to whatever arrangements you make.

❖ If your child wants something expensive and you have no objection to the purchase, ask him to earn and pay for a portion, and agree to cover the rest (to whatever degree you can afford). For example, if he wants designer jeans, you might offer to pay what "regular" jeans would cost and let him make up the difference himself.

❖ If you give, give freely—no lectures about how easy he's got it, how spoiled he is, how hard you had to work for it or how money doesn't grow on trees.

❖ When your child is old enough, help him develop accountability. For example, a lot of children believe that when you want money, all you have to do is go to an ATM and *get* some! Talk to him about how you have to put money *in* first—even show him a bank statement to "prove" that money doesn't just come out of a wall!

❖ Teach your child to save. Start a savings account for your child, and help him plan and commit to a savings program (for example, a portion of his allowance, earnings or gifts). Help him determine the purpose of this account, his savings goals and an acceptable minimum balance (or maximum percentage he may withdraw).

❖ If you agree to lend your child money, ask him how he plans to repay the loan, and even request collateral (siblings not acceptable). Your child may take you more seriously if you get something in writing, even if it's for small amounts.

❖ If you must borrow from your child, give him an IOU or sign some written agreement. Pay him back on time. Model responsible borrowing behavior.

❖ Start small and start young. It's a great way to help teach responsibility!

14 Ways to Encourage Positive Choices for Good Health and Safety

❖ Make good choices yourself. Eat well. Exercise. Quit smoking (or at least quit smoking in the house and the car, particularly when your child is around). Take care of your teeth.

❖ Wear your seat belt. Start the car and drive only when everyone is buckled up.

❖ Minimize the amount of junk food you bring into the house.

❖ Eat at restaurants other than fast-food places, at least once in a while. Make healthy choices wherever you eat.

❖ Model and encourage nonsedentary activities.

❖ Ask your child for input in planning family activities, or things you do one-on-one with your child, that involve something besides TV or video games.

❖ Model and teach habits of personal hygiene. Develop and regularly practice routines like washing your hands before coming to the table and brushing your teeth before bed.

❖ Offer choices of healthy desserts and snacks.

❖ Teach your child to take care of her teeth early on. Take her to the dentist at least once before she has to go as a patient.

❖ Ask your child to agree to give away a portion of the Halloween candy she collects. Take her along to donate the candy to a shelter or community center.

❖ Read labels on packaged foods. Talk to your child about which foods are most natural.

❖ Ask your child to help plan meals. Tell her to make sure she has at least three different colors of food on the plate (using the appropriate food groups).

❖ Teach your child basic first-aid strategies and how (and when) to dial 911 for help.

❖ Teach your child to set and respect limits about her body, to say no to uncomfortable touches, and to differentiate between "telling" (to protect herself or someone else) and "tattling" (to get attention or approval, to get an adult to solve her problems, or to get someone in trouble).

11 Ways to Create Success with Your Baby-Sitter

❖ Either use someone your child already knows or invite your sitter over to meet (and play with) your child ahead of time. (Refer to this person by name, not as "the baby-sitter.") Let your child know that this person will be coming over to stay with him when you go out tomorrow (or in two days, for example).

❖ If your older children aren't quite old enough to leave in charge of younger siblings, allow them to stay with a friend or relative if they don't want to stay home when you hire the sitter.

❖ Leave a list of phone numbers—a neighbor or relative, the police and fire departments, your pager or cellular phone (if you have one), and the number where you'll be. Give instructions on what to do in case of an emergency. Discuss what qualifies as an emergency and under what circumstances you want to be contacted.

❖ Write down any rules or limits you have for your child. (It's harder for your child to argue with something in writing!)

❖ Let sitters know ahead of time which snacks are okay to eat, which rooms are okay to go into, how to run the VCR (although they probably know this better than you) and whether or not they can use the phone, stereo, microwave or computer. Discuss whether or not they can bring a friend over.

❖ If possible, don't plan for anyone to come over while the sitter is there. If you are expecting a delivery, for example, or know that a friend or relative may drop by while you're gone, make sure the sitter knows what to expect and how to handle the situation.

❖ Come home when you say you're going to come home. If you're going to be late, call the sitter with the new time.

❖ Pay on time. If you have to pay late, pay a little more.

❖ If your child will be awake for much of the time your sitter will be there, leave materials for activities your child can do with the sitter or on his own—crayons, paper, books, toys, games or videos, for example. Have lots of things available that your child likes to do.

❖ If the sitter did something extra like cleaning or doing special activities with your child, throw in a little extra pay. (You want to stay on this person's "A-list" of clients!)

❖ If you have to cancel, let your sitter know in enough time to line up another job or something else to do. If you cancel at the last minute, offer to pay at least a part of what you would have paid had he or she actually worked for you.

15 Ways to Minimize Conflicts on Car Trips

❖ Have realistic expectations. Confinement in a small space for any length of time becomes monotonous for kids of all ages (and adults, too), no matter how excited they are about the trip.

❖ Maintain a positive attitude. If you see the trip as an opportunity to share some valuable time with your children, you're bound to inspire more positive expectations than if you anticipate the trip with dread.

❖ Plan to stop often.

❖ Tell your children when you'll get there in terms they can understand: a specific time, when the little hand is on the seven, not until dark, after we stop for dinner.

❖ To discourage fighting over who sits where, prepare a seating chart with rotations at specified intervals.

❖ Take plenty of things for your kids to read, listen to or play with—lots more than you think you'll need. Buy, rent or borrow lots of tapes, books, electronic games, an Etch-a-Sketch, Viewmasters or travel games. Take along a sketch pad (with hard cardboard backing), crayons or markers, stickers, wipe-off books, magazines and activity books, mazes, maps, or even store catalogs to look at.

❖ Draw a map of your route with landmarks, cities, exits or special things for your kid to look for to help track your progress. Make sure each child (if you have more than one) has his or her own copy. (You can also mark the route you plan to take on a commercial map for each child and point out towns, roads, parks, airports or turnoffs that might be on the map.)

❖ Have a scavenger hunt. Before departure, make a list (or draw pictures) of things for each child to look for along the way. Depending on where you're heading, your list might include a red barn, a green truck, a sign that starts with the letter *K,* a purple flower, a drive-in screen, a bicycle, a sheep, a brick building, a school, a flag, a blue neon sign, or a particular store, gas station or restaurant that your children may recognize.

❖ Have storage containers, Ziploc bags, boxes or tote bags for everything you bring.

❖ Tell stories. Ask your kids to tell stories to you.

❖ Use travel time as a chance to share. Talk about a trip you took when you were young. Encourage your kids to talk to you and ask you questions. Ask them questions and listen to what they have to say.

❖ Play games like 20 questions or I-spy. (Research car games before you leave.)

❖ Take along a self-soother like a favorite toy, stuffed animal, blanket or pillow for everyone on the ride.

❖ Take plenty of snacks, juice and water.

❖ Don't forget the wet wipes, Band-Aids, Kleenex, aspirin, trash bag and a sense of humor.

15 Ways to Drug-Proof Your Child*

❖ Recognize that no matter how much you want your child never to try drugs, your ability to control this choice is extremely limited.

❖ Reduce the likelihood of rebellious experimentation by creating a win-win home environment so your child doesn't feel the need to use drugs to prove you can't control her.

❖ Accommodate the need for emotional safety—as well as the need to have and express feelings—so your child isn't tempted to use drugs to escape or become numb.

❖ Accommodate the need for unconditional love and acceptance. (It's nearly impossible to say no to friends when you're used to having to say yes to be safe, loved and accepted at home!)

❖ Talk honestly about drugs. Avoid scare tactics. (Yes, drugs and alcohol can be fun—that's what makes them dangerous.)

---

* Includes helping kids develop resistance to using any mood-altering substance or behavior.

❖ Don't use drugs yourself. (If asked, be honest about past drug use without going into great detail. There's a certain legitimacy to admitting that it's hard for you to ask your child not to do something that you once tried.)

❖ If you do use drugs or alcohol, don't involve your kid by asking her to get you a beer or light your cigarettes for you, for example.

❖ Teach and model assertiveness. Help your kid learn to stand up for herself without having to apologize, defend or make excuses for her choices.

❖ Encourage your child to choose friends who respect her feelings and choices, who love and accept her for who she is—just like you do!

❖ Give your kid lots of opportunities to make decisions and build thinking skills.

❖ Help your child anticipate offers from friends. "What can you say if your friends want you to get high with them?" "What if they make fun of you for refusing (or don't want to be your friend anymore)?"

❖ Encourage participation and involvement in groups, sports and hobbies. (Physical activity can create a great natural "high.")

❖ Emphasize that it's absolutely essential that she call for a ride if she or her friends drink. (Many parents say it works best if you add "No questions asked.")

❖ Try, try, *try* to stay calm and neutral if your child has the courage—and trusts you enough—to admit that she's experimented or is considering it. Help her explore the possible consequences of trying something (or continuing) and of resisting (or quitting). Ask how she'll handle temptation or resist pressure to participate in the future. Ask her if she would like to see a counselor or join a group to talk about what's going on in her life. (Leave the door open for her to change her mind if she says no.) Tell her your preferences and any limits or possible actions you may find necessary to take, and don't be afraid to admit that the final decision—and responsibility—will be hers.

❖ Enjoy the beauty of life's simplicities, and teach your child to do the same.

PART VI

Dealing with Feelings (Supportiveness)

Dealing with Feelings
(Supportiveness)

Most parents I've encountered say they want their kids to come and talk to them when they're in crisis, when they're upset or when they have a problem. But how often do these same parents block the very communication they desire when they inadvertently respond in a way that says it's not safe or okay for their kids to be feeling what they're feeling, or to be upset about what they're upset about?

The quality of the response is often a matter of timing. Children may not get the support they need if parents are distracted, stressed, tired or busy. Kids who have problems that could have easily been avoided if they had made more sensible choices (especially if they had just listened to parents in the first place) may encounter an adult's

impatience, annoyance, disappointment or anger instead
of comfort and validation. And sometimes, the most well
intended responses may work in the interest of time—
offering quick assurances or solutions—without actually
addressing how the kids feel!

Of the lists in this section, only two are situational:
the ones that help kids deal with death and with divorce.
All the others offer suggestions for creating an environment in which feelings are safe to express (in nonhurtful
ways). These lists emphasize good listening, healthy
outlets for anger, what validation looks like, and the
kind of parenting roles, words and attitudes that help
this type of supportive environment develop.

5 Reasons to Help Your Children Learn to Express Their Feelings in Healthy, Nondestructive Ways

❖ Stuffed feelings tend to build up inside, and can end up being expressed reactively and explosively.* (Have you ever seen a child who's been having a bad day suddenly blow up at the slightest offense?)

❖ Stuffed feelings can show up as physical symptoms such as headaches or tummy aches and eventually turn into something more serious.

❖ Stuffed feelings (especially anger) can turn into destructive or self-destructive behaviors.

❖ Drugs, alcohol, food, nicotine and other substances can become very attractive to someone who's trying not to feel something. (It's a lot easier not to feel if you're high.)

---

* The term "stuffed feelings" refers to feelings that are submerged, repressed or discounted when they don't have a way to be expressed or come out, when expressing feelings is discouraged or likely to result in a negative or nonsupportive reaction (such as judgment, ridicule, blaming, criticizing, dismissing, challenging or minimizing), or in response to trauma that is too painful to consciously remember (dissociation).

❖ When kids have a chance to process (feel, express and learn from) their feelings, they are free to deal with the problems or issues related to those feelings in healthier and more positive ways.

17 Ways to Make It Safe for Your Child to Have and Express Feelings

❖ Listen attentively. Minimize the amount of talking you do. Encourage with a few brief comments like "Tell me more" or "What's going on?"

❖ Make eye contact while he's talking. If you're unable to give him your full attention when he wants it, let him know when you *will* be available.

❖ Don't interrupt.

❖ Keep the focus on him. Watch the temptation to start talking about yourself, your feelings or your experiences unless he asks for this kind of feedback.

❖ Remember that feelings are not the same as behaviors. There's a difference between *wanting* to hurt someone when you're angry and actually hurting someone. (It's okay to *want* to punch your sister for breaking your toy; it's not okay to actually do it.)

❖ Give him space just to have his feelings. The need to cheer him up may make *you* feel better, but it probably won't help him in the long run.

❖ Provide nondestructive outlets for feelings. *(See "16 Things You Can Suggest to Help Your Child Let Out Anger Nondestructively" for more information.)*

❖ Don't judge. Feelings are neither right nor wrong. Accept how your child feels, even if it's different from how *you* would respond to the same situation.

❖ Accept his right to his feelings. Avoid judgmental, shocked or disappointed reactions—words, looks or body language. Be careful not to make him think that he's wrong for how he feels.

❖ Resist the urge to challenge his feelings, asking him to defend or explain why he's feeling a certain way. For one thing, he may not know, and even if he does know, he may not be able to put the feelings—or the reason for the feelings—into words. (Feeling and explaining are two different processes.) Also, asking a child to justify why he feels a certain way can suggest that you won't accept his feelings unless he has a good enough reason for them.

❖ Validate his right to have his feelings, even if they don't make sense to you, even if they seem silly or incomprehensible to you. (Validation is anything that gives a child permission to have his feelings: "It can really hurt when someone says that." "Monsters are scary.")

❖ Respect the fact that he may not want to talk about it right now. Tell him he can come to you later if he changes his mind.

❖ Keep in mind that you can be supportive without adopting another person's feelings. You don't have to be sad just because your child is sad.

❖ Stay clear on your role. Supportiveness means listening, accepting and validating. Watch the urge to use these exchanges as an excuse to criticize or give advice. At some point, you can help him explore possible solutions. In the meantime, help him deal with his feelings, rather than focusing on the need to find a solution or fix the situation.

❖ Examine any discomfort, fear or sense of inadequacy you experience when your child exhibits strong feelings. Remember that feelings are a part of being human and being alive. It's neither necessary nor helpful to prevent your child from having feelings, to protect him from uncomfortable feelings, or to "fix" him or his problems when he's upset.

❖ Be aware of any inclination to cave in on your limits to keep your child from getting upset. You can allow your child to have his feelings and still maintain your boundaries: "You can be angry at me for asking you to take a bath. You still have to take a bath" or "Of course you're upset that you can't use the phone. You can use it as soon as you finish your chores."

❖ Model and teach conflict management. Demonstrate healthy ways to have, express and process feelings, to express needs, and to set and maintain boundaries, so that when conflicts occur in your child's life, he'll have an example of how he can do the same.

When children have the emotional space and safety to express feelings nondestructively, they don't have to "stuff" their feelings or pretend that they're "fine," just to protect an anxious adult or avoid the adult's negative reactions.

9 Characteristics of Good Listeners

❖ They don't interrupt.

❖ They don't judge.

❖ They acknowledge what the other person is saying.

❖ They make eye contact.

❖ They say things to encourage the other person to talk and share: "Tell me more," "What happened then?"

❖ They give the person talking their full attention.

❖ They respect the other person's right *not* to share. They leave the door open for a discussion at a later time if the other person wants to talk then.

❖ When they are unavailable or unable to give their full attention, they let the other person know when they'll be free.

❖ They maintain confidentiality and do not repeat anything discussed without the permission of the person they've listened to. If they feel that they will be compelled to break confidentiality, they let the other person know ahead of time.

> "*Listening is the oldest and perhaps the most powerful tool of healing. It is often through the quality of our listening and not the wisdom of our words that we are able to effect the most profound changes in people around us.*"
>
> **—Rachel Naomi Remen, M.D.**

14 Ways to Respect Your Child's Reality

❖ Recognize that we can all experience the same things differently, that the same event can trigger different impressions and perceptions. Respect your child's right to see and experience things differently from you.

❖ Remember that it's okay to simply accept your child's feelings or opinions without agreeing with them or asking her to defend them: "So you think Mrs. White is mean," "You believe his parents acted unfairly" or "You really like this TV show."

❖ Validate your child's feelings and observations: "Of course you're angry about that!" "Yes, it hurts when people call you names" or "I can see that really bothers you." You can support the reality of her experience even if you'd respond differently in the same situation.

❖ Watch out for invalidating statements like "You don't really feel that way," "Big girls aren't afraid of thunder," "That's ridiculous. Your teacher doesn't hate you" or "You're just too sensitive."

❖ When your child can't have her way, validate her desires: "I know you wish you could have candy for breakfast" or "I know you wish you could sleep in Mommy's bed tonight."*

❖ Accept things your child comments on or believes in, even if they aren't real to you (for example, angels, imaginary friends or monsters under the bed).

❖ Respect your child's perspective, even if it's different from yours. Listen to her opinions without judging them (or her). Never laugh at her ideas unless she was trying to be funny.

❖ Take your child seriously, especially when she's upset. Even if you know that "this won't matter" in a few years (or even a few minutes), for the moment, the trauma is very real to her. Respect her right to her feelings even if you think she's overreacting. (In her reality, she isn't.)

❖ Even if she's got it so good (or easy) or has a lot to be grateful for, she's still entitled to her disappointments,

---

* Validating a child's feelings and desires does not give her permission to do what she wants. For example, saying "You really wish you could drop out of school" does not give the child permission to drop out—it just gives her permission to be angry and frustrated.

hurt feelings and heartaches. And if she's lucky, this really *isn't* the best time of her life!

❖ Explain things in terms of your child's experience, using examples from her life: "Remember how you felt when Joey broke your truck? That's how I feel right now."

❖ Encourage your child to trust her instincts and validate them when she does. Respect her inner guidance, sensitivities or general inclinations—whether this means not liking a certain person or choosing to become a vegetarian, for example.

❖ Accept the fact that your child may experience the temperature very differently from you, need less (or more) sleep or food than you think she should have, or not be as much of a "morning person" as you are. Watch the tendency to criticize or try to change these characteristics.

❖ Avoid discouraging dreams or goals, no matter how badly you want to protect your child from the possibility of disappointment, failure or ridicule.

❖ Rather than asking for a "story" to explain how something happened, to identify a scapegoat or to determine "who started it," focus on the solution. Help your child identify what she needs to do to correct what happened or prevent it from happening again. (Whether the bowl was too heavy for her to carry or "a big green dog" chased her and she fell, the child's reality—or the version she shares with you—is not the issue here.)

Allow your child to grow up trusting her feelings, her perceptions and the validity of her own experiences. Watch the tendency to discourage her from valuing different things from you—or the need for her to feel the same way you do about certain things—in order for you to feel okay. You can avoid the conflict and stress of "reality wars" when you're not threatened by differences between you and your child's preferences or beliefs.

16 Things You Can Suggest to Help Your Child Let Out Anger Nondestructively

❖ Stomp your feet and yell! (Perhaps in your room, in the basement or in the garage, if the noise will disturb others.)

❖ Draw a picture of how you feel—or what you *wish* you could do. (Then tear it into 100 pieces.)

❖ Talk into a tape recorder about how you feel. (Then erase the tape.)

❖ Make a noise that sounds like how you feel.

❖ Pound on a pillow, a punching bag or the cushions on the couch. (It's even okay to pretend the pillow is the person!)

❖ Go for a walk or a run.

❖ Talk about your feelings to a parent, a friend or your dog.

❖ Take a few deep breaths. (Blowing bubbles works great for this!)

❖ Have a good cry. Throw a tantrum.

❖ Talk to a stuffed animal or a pillow about how you feel. Pretend the toy is the person you're angry at or a friend who will let you say whatever you want and keep your secret forever.

❖ Pound on clay.

❖ Take a warm bath to "wash away the mad feelings."

❖ Kick a soccer ball or football.

❖ Clean something. (Scrubbing is a wonderful outlet!)

❖ Write a letter to the person you're angry at. Tear it up and throw it out when you're through.

❖ Write in your journal.

Remember, the point is to help your child get the anger out of his system in some way that will not hurt him or anyone else, and to communicate that it's okay to feel angry. Caution: Certain ideas suit certain children better. If a particular activity seems to prolong or intensify the anger instead of releasing it, switch to something else!

12 Things *Never* to Say When Your Child's Feelings Have Been Hurt

❖ "What did you do to *her?*"

❖ "Sticks and stones may break my bones, but words will never hurt me."

❖ "He didn't mean it."

❖ "That's nothing to be upset about."

❖ "You're just too sensitive."

❖ "You think *you've* got problems."

❖ "Cheer up! This is the best time of your life."

❖ "You're lucky you have any friends."

❖ "Don't be such a baby."

❖ "Big girls don't cry."

❖ "Why does that bother you?"

❖ "I'll bet some ice cream would make you feel better."

Trying to cheer your child up or make the feelings go away, making her wrong for having feelings, asking her to defend or explain her feelings, or trying to fix the problem is not supportive. These responses deny your child the opportunity to work through the feelings in a safe, supportive emotional environment.

(See "5 Reasons to Help Your Children Learn to Express Their Feelings in Healthy, Nondestructive Ways," "17 Ways to Make It Safe for Your Child to Have and Express Feelings," "9 Characteristics of Good Listeners" and "14 Ways to Respect Your Child's Reality" for alternatives.)

13 Ways to Help Your Child Deal with Death or Loss

❖ Answer questions as simply and honestly as possible. If you're not prepared to answer your child's inquiries, tell him you need a little time to think about it first.

❖ Together, read and discuss a book that addresses these issues from a child's point of view. (Ask a librarian, a bookstore owner, a teacher or another adult who may have encountered these questions to recommend a few titles to you.)

❖ Resist the impulse to try to protect your child from the realities of life. Allow and encourage your child to visit aging relatives and family friends, to see people at all stages of life.

❖ Let your child see the real emotions that accompany death and loss, and the rituals that go with it. Don't be afraid to let your child see you grieve.

❖ Explain that the love and connection you feel for someone, and the memories you will always have, go on forever, even though that person is gone. (The same goes for pets, too.)

❖ It often helps to talk about positive memories: "What did you love best about Grandpa?" or "What was the best time you ever spent with him?" Commemorating a loved one can help your child resolve grief, look back with joy and move ahead enriched by the experience.

❖ Validate your child's feelings about the person (or pet) who died: "You really loved her, didn't you?"

❖ Allow your child to "live his pain," to feel his loss and discuss his feelings. Be there for him as much as you are able. Let him cry. Hold him if he wants to be held.

❖ Give him space to talk about his feelings, but respect his right to keep his feelings private if he needs to.

❖ Keep in mind that children may have a hard time expressing abstract feelings, especially in the same words adults use. (Some children can express their feelings better by drawing, writing in a journal, telling a story, or playing with puppets or dolls.)

❖ At different ages, children have different ways of understanding death, different fears and different questions. It's natural for your child to feel confused, angry, vulnerable, frightened or even guilty. Offer as much reassurance as possible at this time, enlisting the help of family, friends, a counselor or a support group as necessary to help *you* support your child.

❖ Understand that everyone grieves differently and that the length of time to work through a loss will vary from person to person and event to event. Watch for your own impatience for your child to "just get over it" or the temptation to rush your child through the process.

❖ If you notice changes in eating or sleeping patterns that go on for more than two or three weeks, or if you notice persistent hyperactivity (wildness or frenetic behavior) or increased anger, defiance or destructiveness, your child may be experiencing depression—not just grief or sadness. Some children need more than the family can provide at this time to help process their feelings. Consider the services of a skilled play therapist or a counselor who is used to dealing with children.

17 Ways to Help Your Children Survive Your Divorce

❖ Maintain a civil relationship with your spouse* during the divorce and afterward. Treat each other with tolerance and respect.

❖ Don't bad-mouth your spouse to your children regardless of your feelings for him or her, and regardless of anything your spouse did during your marriage. (It's tempting to want to make the other person look bad to rationalize leaving—or being left.)

❖ Take care of yourself. Get good legal representation or mediation, even if your spouse swears he or she wants a friendly divorce. Divorce can be a lot less traumatic for everyone when you can take care of your children financially and provide a stable residence for them.

❖ Keep your kids out of the middle of your divorce. Don't ask them to take messages back and forth. Talk to your spouse directly (or through your attorney).

---

* Ex-spouse or former partner.

❖ Don't try to make your children your friends or lean on them for support. Reach out to adult friends or family members, a counselor, or a group to help you through.

❖ Don't ask your children to choose between you and your spouse. Ever.

❖ Talk to your children when both parents are there. Without blaming or getting angry, tell the children what's happening (and what's going to happen). Reassure them that this has nothing to do with them and that *it isn't their fault.*

❖ Stay as close to your kids as possible. Be there for them. Even older children may imagine that "my parents don't love each other, so they must not love me." Tell them that you love them and that you'll be there for them. Reassure them often.

❖ Don't talk to other adults in front of your children about the horrible things that went on in your marriage.

❖ Listen to your children with an open mind. Respect their feelings about your spouse and about the divorce itself.

❖ Take time for your children. Keep doing the fun things that you used to do with them.

❖ Don't talk about the divorce constantly. Let your children bring it up when they need to talk about it. Don't prod them to talk about it when they don't want to.

❖ Encourage your children to respect and honor the other parent, even if you can't get along with your spouse. (Many children feel they have to hate one parent to protect, comfort or prove loyalty to the other. Keep children out of the battle zone. It serves no one.)

❖ Unless their safety is clearly at risk, encourage your children to have their own relationship with your spouse and to keep it separate from their relationship with you.

❖ Resist using your children to find out about what your spouse is doing, whom your spouse is dating, or what your spouse's new house is like. (Many divorced parents specifically ask their children *not* to tell them about their ex-spouse's life and request that the children respect their privacy as well.)

❖ Avoid discussing money issues with your children or blaming financial problems on your spouse, even if it's true. Rather than "Well, if your dad had paid child support, we could get that for you," try "We can't afford that right now."

❖ Watch the inclination to overcompensate by indulging your children or buying them things so that you'll feel less guilty. Forgive yourself.

PART VII

Healthy
Parenting
(Personal
Issues and
Self-Care)

Healthy Parenting
(Personal Issues and Self-Care)

The process of interacting with other people offers continual opportunities to grow, to learn new skills, to uncover and heal old hurts. On an off-day, even people we don't know (or don't know well) can trigger hurt feelings, anger, or a sense of embarrassment with a well-timed comment or look. So imagine how well-equipped your own child is to mirror any issues you may have about things like power and control, respect and approval, the need to feel important and valued, or how you "look" as a parent.

This section includes lists about "grown-up topics" to help you in your personal development and self-care as a parent. Many of these suggestions focus on preventing problems or becoming more aware of your own choices and actions. In some cases, you'll find ways to deal with unpleasant behaviors or comments, or the feelings that your child's behavior may trigger for you. Other lists offer ways to examine conflicts and learn from them, ideas on time management and changing the way your family operates, and a lot of great things about your child at specific ages.

In the section that follows this one there are topics to help you create your own lists—and in the process, examine your own priorities, values, goals and successes. I hope that these and the other lists in this book contribute to the ongoing development of a lifelong, happy, fulfilling and loving relationship between you and your child.

14 Ways to Become a More Conscious Parent*

❖ Identify your parenting goals. Think of what you want your relationship to be like and what you can do to make that happen. Look at both long-term and short-term objectives.

❖ Make a little sign for yourself that says "My relationship with my child(ren) is important. What I do and say matters." Leave this note in a place where you can see it as you start your day. It can help you remember to pay attention to how you interact.

❖ Pray for awareness (or ask for inner guidance) to stay conscious of how you act around and with your children.

❖ Ask yourself "What can I do today to invest in the quality of this relationship?"

---

* The suggestions in this list are meant to help you grow in your awareness of your parenting behaviors and to be as "present" as possible in your interactions with your children, rather than just relying on reflex or automatic behaviors, attitudes, expectations and language patterns.

❖ Affirm that you are becoming a more conscious parent. Create a meaningful and relevant statement you can repeat at the beginning and end of the day, and as often as necessary in between: "I am parenting more consciously all the time" or "I think before I talk to my child." Even if the statement isn't true at the moment, say it as though it were!

❖ Throughout the day, take a few seconds for yourself to deliberately get grounded, focused, more present or more relaxed. A few deep breaths and a minute or two alone, if possible, can really help.

❖ Ask your child for feedback. Focus on the positive: "What am I doing that helps you?" or "What am I doing great?"

❖ Listen to your children and really hear what they say. Take your children's comments seriously.

❖ Don't just watch your children—really *be* with them as they explore their world.

❖ Read children's books. Watch movies made for children. Play with your child's games and toys.

❖ When you blow it, think of specific ways you can behave more constructively next time. (It may help if you write down your intentions.) Use your guilt to change your behavior, not as an excuse to beat your-self up, get discouraged or give up.

❖ Keep a journal. Take a few minutes for yourself and make the time to write. (Journals are great places to work through feelings, reactions and fears, and to keep track of events as well as successes and growth.)

❖ Make time for yourself, for noticing what you need and for giving to yourself. *(See "6 Ways to Take More Time for Yourself" for more information.)*

❖ Note your successes. Before you go to bed, think of at least three things you did well or better that day. Write them down on a notepad or calendar, in a date book or "progress journal." Don't qualify your suc-cesses—just focus on what you did right!

It will always be easier to automatically slip into patterns you know best, especially if you've had a long day or feel overwhelmed by life's little distractions and problems. However, becoming more conscious of what you bring to your relationships tends to enhance the quality of your rela-tionships, strengthens a belief in your ability to make changes in your life and puts you in a position to make more constructive choices when opportunities arise.

9 Ways to Be More Proactive*

❖ Write down your parenting goals. Be specific about behaviors, principles and long-term outcomes that are important to you. It's easier to anticipate, plan and prevent problems when you know what you're trying to achieve!

❖ Involve your children in discussions of your family's goals, values and priorities.

❖ Review your parenting goals from time to time. Keep your long-range goals in mind, especially when dealing with day-to-day issues and events.

❖ Think prevention! Focus on encouraging positive behavior rather than looking for ways to punish or react to misbehavior.

❖ Anticipate what you'll want in various situations. Anticipate what your children will want in those situations. Look for ways to accommodate both sets of needs.

---

* Proactivity is a positive alternative to reactivity. It involves the ability to *prevent* problems by anticipating and accommodating needs, to deal with potential conflicts before they actually occur, and often, to respond to negative behaviors in more positive (less reactive) ways.

❖ Communicate the kind of behavior you're looking for. Ask for what you want. Be specific and clear.

❖ Respond to misbehavior less reactively. Use conflicts as opportunities to learn new approaches or ways to prevent further conflict.

❖ Look for solutions, not blame.

❖ Remember that all behaviors happen in the context of your relationship. Keep the emphasis on the relationship—hopefully, it will be there long after a particular behavior is no longer an issue.

4 Ways to Avoid Operating on a Double Standard

❖ Hold yourself to the same standards as those which you hold for your children. Model the kind of behaviors and values you want your children to develop. Let them see you being honest, responsible, neat, punctual, curious, respectful, polite, kind, patient, considerate, self-disciplined and self-caring. Let them see you own up to your mistakes, repair or replace things you break, and ask for information or help when you need it. Let them see your resistance to blaming, compromising your integrity or taking the easy way out.

❖ Notice how you talk to your children. Make sure your behaviors, language, attitude, tone of voice and body language are congruent with what you want and would tolerate from your children. (Talk to your children with the same respect and consideration you'd summon for an adult you really valued.)

❖ Notice the things your children do that bother you. Would you really hassle an adult for eating all his peas first to get them out of the way, for putting ketchup on his fries instead of on the side, or for wanting to wear the same color every day?

❖ Remember that your children need and respond to positive motivation—just like you do.

18 Characteristics of Parents at Risk*

❖ They feel personally responsible for their children's successes and failures.

❖ They measure personal adequacy and success by their children's behavior and achievement or by the approval they get from others.

❖ They need to avoid conflict and gain other people's approval to a degree that can undermine or interfere with their ultimate parenting goals.

❖ They compromise (or even violate) their children's needs in order to avoid "rocking the boat," or to look good to a parenting partner or some other adult.

❖ They are discouraged, disempowered or vindicated by the belief that their job as a parent would be easier to perform if only the children (or the spouse, the grandparents, the children's friends, the school or teachers) would change.

---

* At risk for stress and conflict; feelings of frustration, disempowerment, helplessness, resentment, rage, insecurity or self-doubt; fear of rejection or disapproval (inadequacy); depression, illness, exhaustion, competitiveness, addictive or compulsive "coping" behavior, or an overwhelming sense of responsibility for everyone and everything.

❖ They have difficulty setting and maintaining boundaries between themselves and other people.

❖ They have difficulty setting and maintaining boundaries between themselves and their work.

❖ They deal with discipline problems by shaming, blaming, complaining, manipulating, ignoring them or dumping them on someone else ("Wait till your father gets home!").

❖ They feel threatened by the progress or success of their parenting partner or other parents.

❖ They often feel as though "things would completely fall apart if it weren't for me."

❖ They swing from feelings of helplessness and victimization to moral superiority and self-righteousness.

❖ They may measure their devotion or validate their commitment to their children by how much they give, give up or suffer.

❖ They have difficulty saying no.

❖ They often enable their children by ignoring misbehavior, by offering inappropriate second chances or by failing to impose previously stated consequences.

❖ They may protect their children from failure or negative consequences in an effort to feel successful,
   valuable, important or powerful.

❖ They overidentify with, and even adopt, their children's feelings.

❖ They are heavily invested in appearing to be "fine"
   and "in control."

❖ They would probably deny that any of the above are
   true or personally relevant.

We're probably all guilty, to some degree, of all of the
above from time to time. However, if many of the above
characteristics describe your feelings, beliefs and behaviors
much of the time, you're probably experiencing more stress
in your life than you would like. The other lists in this book can
help you find more productive ways to relate to others, particularly your children and family.

8 Ways to Deal with Your Child's Saying "I Hate You!"

❖ Keep in mind that a child usually says "I hate you" when he knows it will meet his need for attention or control. Resist the urge to react, change your child's mind or give your child what he wants so he won't hate you. The less impressed you are, the sooner he'll recognize that this strategy doesn't work, and the sooner he'll quit trying to manipulate your feelings and behaviors by saying "I hate you."

❖ Don't take it personally. (Of course, this statement may very well trigger anger, shame, shock, fear or a sense of inadequacy. It's supposed to.)

❖ Acknowledge your child's feelings: "I understand you're angry about this" or "You must be pretty upset that you can't have this right now."

❖ Resist the temptation to hurt back. Your child needs a stable adult. Saying "Well, I hate you, too, sometimes!" may be exactly what you're feeling at the moment, but it won't help you, your child, your relationship or the situation.

❖ Don't shame your child for saying "I hate you," even if you believe the behavior is wrong. Your child probably has limited strategies for expressing feelings. Making him feel he is wrong for being angry may simply compound the problem. (And if he's acting out for attention, even this negative attention will reinforce his behavior!)

❖ If you find yourself getting really upset, try to disengage.* If necessary, walk away, leaving the door open for further discussion at a later, calmer time: "Let's talk about this in a little bit." *(See "10 Ways to Avoid Getting Hooked by Your Child's Misbehavior" and "7 Ways You Can Constructively Deal with Your Child's Abusive or Obnoxious Behavior" for more information.)*

❖ Talk to some supportive adult if feelings of panic or anger come up when you hear this statement. Be careful not to burden your child with your emotional trauma by saying something like "When you say that, I feel scared, hurt and angry!" Whatever you're feeling has very little to do with him.

❖ Do something to remind yourself that you are lovable and wonderful, no matter what your child says!

---

* This means to separate—emotionally and sometimes physically—to pull back, unhook or get free from the interaction.

10 Ways to Avoid Getting Hooked by Your Child's Misbehavior

❖ Pick your fights carefully. (Will this really matter 10 years from now?) Try to keep the big picture—your relationship—in mind.

❖ Avoid getting stuck on needing to be right or needing to win.

❖ Depersonalize conflicts. Your child may do dumb things out of curiosity, creativity, a lack of experience or perspective, a failure to think things through, or just because it sounded "cool" at the time. In most cases, her choices were probably not intended to hurt you or make you look bad.

❖ Do not act impressed or shocked by attention-getting behavior. Ask for what you want instead: "Please don't use that word around me" or "We don't do (or say) that in our home." Give as little attention and as few words as possible to this type of misbehavior.

❖ Beware of the tendency to make decisions or compromise your values (or boundaries) in order to gain your child's approval or to avoid her negative reaction (crying, begging, tantrum or any kind of acting out). Let it be okay for her to be upset when she doesn't get her way.

❖ When your child gets upset with you, acknowledge her feelings: "You sound really angry right now." Rather than getting defensive or scolding her for getting upset, tell her under what conditions you'll be willing to give her what she wants, or what options are available.

❖ Look at the misbehavior as an opportunity for your child to learn to make better choices next time, instead of using it as an opportunity to scold, shame, fight, be disappointed or make your child wrong.

❖ Trust your child's ability to rebound from a poor decision and to learn from the experience.

❖ Examine how much your own sense of adequacy and success depends upon your child looking or acting a certain way.

❖ Remember that you can do all the "right" things and that your child will still make poor choices. (Sometimes no amount of directions, preparation or warnings can protect her from that urge to see if the paint really *is* wet.)

7 Ways You Can Constructively Deal with Your Child's Abusive or Obnoxious Behavior

❖ Start with your own behavior. Have you modeled the behavior your child is now demonstrating? Have you tolerated this kind of treatment in the past, either from your child or someone else? Identify and practice more positive alternatives.

❖ Say "Wait a minute! Do I talk to you that way?" (This only works if you normally don't use the language, tone or attitude your child is using.) Ask him to "try that again in a different tone of voice." Or ask "How can you say that more respectfully?"

❖ Stay calm. Resist the urge to respond with anger, criticism or moral superiority. However, absolutely refuse to accept abusive behavior or participate in abusive interactions.

❖ If your child refuses to speak or behave more respectfully, set a clear boundary: "Let's try this later. I want to hear what you have to say when you can tell me without yelling." Then walk away.

❖ Give your child space to get his anger or frustration out in a nonhurtful way. Make yourself available to talk when he can interact more peacefully with you.

❖ Avoid telling your child how much it hurts when he yells. This may simply reinforce what he's trying to accomplish. (You want him to change his behavior in order to continue the discussion and be a little more civilized—not to protect your feelings.)

❖ Stay focused on finding a solution that works for everyone. Consider seeking help or mediation if you feel stuck or frustrated, or if the pattern persists.

In a win-win environment, out-of-control, abusive behavior is rare. (A child does not need to resort to this type of behavior to get his needs met.) When a child's anger threatens his own safety or the safety of another person, a pet or property, immediate intervention is essential. However, this is a survival reaction that does not deal with the root of the problem. These behaviors signal the need to examine and restructure family dynamics, particularly if these outbursts occur with any regularity. You will need time, patience, faith and commitment—and possibly some outside help, at least in the beginning.

13 Arguments for *Not* Hitting Your Child*

❖ Using parenting skills like modeling, communication, positivity, encouragement, negotiation, acknowledgment, supportiveness, boundary setting and follow-through—along with having healthy, nondestructive outlets for your anger or rage—can help you achieve your goals and get what you want without hitting your child.

❖ Many parents raise responsible, cooperative, well-adjusted and self-managing children without ever raising a hand to them. (Although all admit to being tempted at times!)

❖ Hitting teaches that physical power is an appropriate way to deal with anger, frustration or annoyance at another person's behavior, particularly if that person is smaller or weaker. It's a great way to teach your child to hit.

❖ Hitting reinforces the need to use violence to get what you want.

---

* Spanking is hitting.

❖ Hitting is a win-lose response to conflict.

❖ Hitting motivates with fear, which compromises your child's emotional safety.

❖ Hitting encourages lying because the threat to your child's physical safety will encourage her to be dishonest to protect herself.

❖ Hitting focuses on "payment" for a misdeed, rather than emphasizing the need to correct mistakes or change behavior.

❖ Hitting encourages your child to be sneakier about her behavior. The emphasis is on avoiding pain rather than committing to more positive behavior.

❖ Hitting is a short-term reaction that sacrifices processes (like working through problems or rethinking behaviors) for an immediate outcome. It can have long-term negative effects on the relationship.

❖ Eventually, the competition for control (and your child's need to "win") may force you to become even more aggressive or to give up altogether.

❖ Compared with hitting, nonviolent consequences (especially restrictions on positive outcomes) teach your child much more effectively that her current

behaviors are not working for her. There are better
incentives for her to change her behavior.

❖ One day your child will be big enough to hit back
(physically and emotionally).

4 Ways to Manage Your Anger*

❖ Physically separate yourself from your child, especially if you're in danger of losing control. Tell him that you're too angry to discuss this right now, that you need a few minutes to cool down before continuing. If you can leave your child alone in the house or in the care of other family members who are present, going for a walk may help you regain some perspective. (Before you leave, reassure your child that you'll be back.)

❖ Do something physical (to something besides your child or yourself). Punch a pillow. Run the vacuum cleaner. Scrub a floor. Go to your room, shut the door, lie on your bed and throw a tantrum. Go into the car, roll up the windows and scream at the top of your lungs. (You may want to drive to an isolated place first.) One parent took out her anger on some bread dough that needed to be kneaded anyhow.

---

* Without hurting your child or yourself.

❖ Get your anger out on paper. Write in your journal or on a notepad. (If you can't think of anything to say, just write, "I'm *so* angry right now!" over and over until something else comes to you.) Write a letter to your child and tear it into 100 pieces when you're finished. Draw a picture of how you feel.

❖ Make contact. Call someone who will listen without criticizing or judging, someone who will understand and accept you, no matter how crazy you feel. (This is especially important if you find that your anger triggers bouts of compulsive or self-destructive behavior.) Consider joining a group of other parents who are willing to share their similar experiences and solutions.

If you do act on your anger, do *not* blame your angry words or behaviors on your child, as in "You make me so mad" or "If you hadn't done that, I wouldn't have hit you." If you say or do something hurtful, apologize without making excuses: "Whoa! That wasn't okay. I'm sorry I said that" or "Wow. I'm really sorry. Can we try that again?" Remember, this is probably what you want your child to do when he hurts someone.

13 Questions That Can Help You Learn from a Conflict with Your Child

❖ "Why am I getting so upset?"

❖ "What's at stake here?"

❖ "How do I feel threatened by my child's behavior?" (Or "What feels threatened in this situation?")

❖ "How is my own behavior contributing to this conflict?"

❖ "What would happen if my child didn't do what I want?"

❖ "What am I really afraid of?"

❖ "What am I trying to accomplish here?"

❖ "How would I handle this situation if it involved someone else's child?"

❖ "How would I handle this situation if it involved another adult instead of my child?"

❖ "If I were my child's age, what would I want in this situation?"

❖ "How can I motivate more cooperative behavior?"

❖ "What can I learn from this experience?"

❖ "If this same situation comes up again, how might I handle it differently next time?"

9 Things You Can Say to Detach from Unsolicited Advice or Criticism About Your Parenting Skills

❖ "You could be right." Then change the subject.

❖ "Thank you for sharing." Then change the subject.

❖ "No kidding." Then change the subject.

❖ "Boy, I was just thinking that myself." Then change the subject.

❖ "I appreciate your concern." Then change the subject.

❖ "It certainly looks like that, doesn't it?" Then change the subject.

❖ "Oh, we don't have to talk about that right now." Then change the subject.

❖ "I must have been absent that day." Then change the subject.

❖ "Really! Don't get me started!" Then change the subject.

Sometimes the best way to defuse a potential conflict is to simply *agree* with the other person. Watch the tendency to become defensive, make excuses, accuse the other person of being nosy or invasive, or make explanations to secure the other person's approval. Changing the subject makes it clear that you don't care to discuss the problem further.

"Instead of being angry or resentful when someone tries to tell you how to live your life, simply listen, bless them and do what your inner self tells you is right."

—**Rev. Norma Hawkins**

10 Things to Remember About Changing Family Dynamics

❖ Family dynamics—specific patterns and behaviors in interactions between family members—are not likely to change all by themselves, even if you have the highest expectations or the best intentions.

❖ Change happens best when you have a sense of what kind of relationship you're trying to create. Identifying your parenting goals gives you a direction to work toward.

❖ Change is most effective when individuals take responsibility for their own growth, rather than attempting to change or blame others. Change is most effective when encouraged rather than coerced.

❖ Kids do what works, even if their behavior seems to generate hurtful or negative outcomes. If you want your children to behave differently, look for ways *you* are willing to change your own behaviors. Kids rarely change until the adults change.

❖ Change happens best in environments that offer emotional safety, acceptance, love, patience and understanding. However, it is possible to adopt healthy patterns of behavior, even in unhealthy and non-supportive environments.*

❖ Change requires consciousness. Awareness of intentions and actual behaviors is the first step toward change.

❖ Consciousness is one of the first casualties of stress, exhaustion and the details of daily life. Commit to a few minutes each day (or even each week) to reflect on how you're doing, what went well, what you might try next (or do differently), and whether or not your goals are still appropriate and meaningful for you.

❖ Sometimes things get worse before they get better.

❖ As individuals change, the system will change.

❖ Change is a process. Relationships, especially relationships with a history of stress and conflict, take time to heal. If you're both still breathing, there's hope. Don't give up. Don't ever give up.

---

* The presence of a supportive parenting partner who shares your beliefs, priorities, values and parenting behaviors is certainly helpful, but not essential, for your attempts at change to be successful. Find support outside the family, if possible. Focus on your own behavior and know that change can happen despite a resistant, unwilling, absent or even addicted partner.

10 Ways to Respect Your Parents as Grandparents

❖ Try not to go crazy over how patiently your parents tolerate behaviors in your child that used to enrage them when you did the same things. Your child will probably experience your parents very differently from the way you did as a child.

❖ Schedule visits that won't tax your (or their) ability to cope. Even if you've *always* gone for two weeks, maybe a weekend would be wiser. (It's more enjoyable when everyone leaves feeling like they would like more time together soon!)

❖ Make sure everyone has some time and space to be alone. A little togetherness goes a long way. (If necessary, wait until you can afford a motel or a separate beach house before getting together.)

❖ Respect the fact that your parents may have outgrown the amount of noise and clutter you're used to, that they may want to get up at a different time or that they may get tired more quickly than you remember.

❖ Respect the fact that your parents may want space and time to themselves, especially if they live nearby. For some grandparents, any opportunity to baby-sit or spend time with the grandchildren is a privilege. For others, it may be a burden or an inconvenience. Don't assume—ask. Make it okay for them to say "no."

❖ Give your parents a little leeway as far as spoiling or indulging your child a bit. Staying up a few minutes later or eating a gooey snack you would never allow in your house can make for special memories for your child without undermining your authority. (Children learn early on that different people have different rules. They're a lot more flexible than we sometimes give them credit for being.)

❖ Don't wait for holidays or special occasions. Video-tape the day-to-day events in your child's life and encourage your parents to reciprocate so your child can get to know them better. Send a giant card, a long sheet of butcher paper rolled up, or an audiocassette with messages or stories from everyone in the family—just to say hi!

❖ Ask your parents to tell your child stories about when you were a child.

❖ Try not to get in the middle of conflicts between your parents and your child. Encourage and help them to work things out with each other.

❖ Don't force a relationship. Give your child opportunities to talk or write to her grandparents and encourage her to stay in touch because she wants to, not because she's supposed to.

26 of the Best Things About Having Two-Year-Olds in Families

❖ They can tell you what's wrong, what's bothering them or why they are crying.

❖ They are inquisitive, humorous, sensitive, imitative, resilient, responsive, affectionate, eager, playful, forceful, unbigoted, pensive, exacting, imaginative, curious, helpful, observant and forgiving.

❖ They provide the perfect opportunity to test and examine the extent of your patience, flexibility and ability to let go of your perfectionism.

❖ By the day—by the minute—you can see them developing the personality and independence to deal with the world on their terms. You can watch their cognitive and verbal abilities grow at an amazing rate!

❖ Their laughter! They know how to fully experience joy.

❖ There is no need to buy expensive toys when there are things like pots and pans, cans or empty boxes to play with.

❖ The look on their faces when they are in the middle of exploration and discovery.

❖ They look at trees, airplanes, birds, bugs, mud, water and everything else with wonder and excitement. Everything is new, and their excitement is contagious!

❖ They make you look at everything like you're seeing it for the first time. They help you see how exciting the learning process really is as you watch their wonderful, curious minds grasp what a world of choices they have at their fingertips.

❖ How much they love themselves! They truly know how to celebrate themselves. They have no problem saying what they love about themselves or what they are good at.

❖ The joy of seeing them eating regular food, being potty trained or putting themselves back to sleep when they wake up during the night.

❖ They can express their feelings without holding back or holding on. They can help you learn how to express feelings and let go of negativity quickly.

❖ They provide you with an opportunity to play with toys that weren't available when you were young.

❖ You hear from them all the words *you* never say in public but that *they* say in the mall, in church or in front of their grandparents.

❖ They are excited to see you after you've been away on a long trip (or just at work for the day).

❖ They give you a great excuse for crawling into bed and napping on a cool, damp afternoon.

❖ Their remarkable confidence! They think they are as old and smart as their parents—just a bit shorter! They are torn between what they think they can do and what they are able to do.

❖ Making a commitment not to spank them can make you a more creative person, challenging you to discover unorthodox ways to get what you want. (For example, one mother found that if she called her daughter, the child was likely to go in the opposite direction. However, if Mom walked backward, her child often came running *to* her, laughing all the way!)

❖ They give parents the chance to begin that hobby or collection they always wanted. ("Really . . . he will love collecting baseball cards when he's 13.")

❖ They are usually welcome at Grandma's house for just about as long as it takes to see a movie or make a quick shopping trip to the mall.

❖ Most of the time, they don't really care if the pants match the shirt when all the coordinated outfits are in the dirty laundry basket.

❖ You know there's a problem any time it gets very, very quiet in the room they are in.

❖ If they nap in the car, you can still carry them into the house, and 9 times out of 10, they will stay asleep.

❖ They make such creative messes!

❖ "I love you, Mommy!" and "I love you, Daddy!" roll easily off their tongues—and they mean it.

❖ They are so cuddly and lovable.

I've included this list to dispel the myth of the "terrible two's." This life stage has received a bad rap, mostly because it's a time when, in developmentally normal children, the desire for power and autonomy first becomes apparent. Rather than fight for control, give your two-year-old some solid, acceptable choices to meet power needs, encourage cooperation and build decision-making capabilities. Then sit back and enjoy the magic of this time in your child's life!

"The way a two-year-old discovers the world where adults have all the answers is similar to the way an adult discovers the world where God has all the answers."

—**Tasneem Virani**
parent educator

18 of the Best Things About Having a Teenager in the Family

❖ They have minds of their own and do not hesitate to voice their opinions.

❖ Their opinions and ideas can be remarkably useful. (And they are so proud when you implement their suggestions!)

❖ At times, you may quiver at the sound of their voices or shrink back into a corner when someone asks "Are they yours?" But just then they say something so profoundly intelligent, or they express an appreciation for something that is really important to you—and that's so satisfying!

❖ Their infrequent compliments of you as a parent mean more than winning the state lottery.

❖ You only have a few years left until their legal independence.

❖ They have all the energy in the world and are simply looking for a place to spend it.

❖ When they say "Let's talk," you know your time will not be wasted.

❖ They allow you to have another friend in the world.

❖ Just when you think they weren't listening to you, they repeat, word-for-word, all your "parentisms."

❖ They are a constant reflection of how well you engage in verbal and nonverbal conversation.

❖ They will push all your buttons, trigger all your character flaws and give you lots of opportunities to work on your own issues.

❖ Because they have sincere and curious minds, they provide continual learning opportunities to parents who are open to growth.

❖ They know they are in the midst of holding onto everything they know about life while trying to let go enough to find what their future holds.

❖ They have opportunities to become anything they want to be if they work hard and have enough desire.

❖ Having long talks about everything, exchanging makeup tips, wearing each other's shoes, cooking together, letting you help them learn to be independent but still needing to have you around.

❖ They sometimes have friends who are more interesting and intelligent than a lot of adults.

❖ Seeing them discover that the world is a little tougher
  than the "complete freedom" they imagine their parents enjoy.

❖ Being able to let go a little. Watching them incorpo-
  rate all that you've taught them and seeing them
  experiment with their own value systems.

Teenagers may be the most underappreciated human
beings on the planet. I've seen parents panic as even the
nicest, most cooperative children approach their 13th
birthday. There are wonderful advantages to having a teen
in your life and many ways in which these years can be
truly *terrific!*

*"The greatest thing about having children is seeing
yourself at their age. Having children is the most personally
enriching experience of my life, bar none."*

—**Dave Hinckley**
parent of two teens

10 Ways to Make More Time for Your Child

❖ Make sure that spending time with your child is a priority. If it isn't, he'll be grown and out of the house before you even realize what you've missed!

❖ Put the things that keep you from spending time with your child in the context of the relationship you want with him—now and in the future.

❖ Say you need the exercise and offer to play basketball or go for a walk together.

❖ Ask your child to help you learn a computer program or how to Rollerblade.

❖ Ask your child to explain (or demonstrate) how he did something.

❖ Set aside time in your schedule *just* for your child. Make "appointments" to spend time with him when it's convenient for both of you.

❖ Encourage your child to spend time with you by doing things he enjoys, by not taking him away from his friends or other things that are important to him, and by keeping the time together positive and easy.

❖ Cook together. (Make something your child really likes.)

❖ "Buddy up" to do some of your chores and your child's chores together.

❖ Have a "just-you-two" day, a day for you and your child to spend together. Allow your child to choose the activity for just you two, such as a movie, a trip to the library, shopping or lunch at his favorite restaurant. Make sure each child in the family has a chance to have a "just-you-two" day, even older children!

"Have you ever noticed how you can spend a half-hour discouraging your child from interrupting you, when giving him a minute or two of your attention, being with him completely and fully for that brief amount of time, will satisfy him? It only takes a few minutes, and they usually run off happily to play. You'll actually create more time for yourself. . . ."

—Deborah Critzer
parent educator

6 Ways to Take More Time for Yourself

❖ When your children are young, start building their independence so they learn to give you some space. Start by spending one minute in a separate room or part of the house—or less if you have to. Add a little more time each day until you work up to what feels like a reasonable break.

❖ Let your children know when you need a few minutes to yourself. Validate their need for your attention and tell them specifically when you'll be available: "I really want to hear about this. I'll be able to listen a whole lot better in 10 minutes (or when the timer goes off, or when this show is over, or when the big hand is on the six)."

❖ If your children are around while you're taking time for yourself, tell them what they're allowed to do and where they're allowed to be while you're in the next room (or your bedroom or the tub, for example). If necessary, make arrangements with an older child in the neighborhood to come over to watch your kids for a few minutes.

❖ Start a baby-sitting co-op with two or three other parents in your community. Plan to take their children for a couple hours a week to give them some free time, in exchange for your kids' staying with them to allow you a few hours to yourself.

❖ Hire a sitter. If money is a problem, volunteer a small portion of the time you take for yourself to run an errand for the person watching your children.

❖ If you have a parenting partner, request a commitment from him or her to spend time with the kids without you, preferably on a regular basis (like every Tuesday from 7:00 until 10:00).

Sometimes the biggest obstacle to taking time for yourself is guilt! Leaving your children in competent hands so that you can get away gives you a chance to "replenish the well." Take care of yourself.

---

36 Things You Can Do to Feel Great!

- ❖ Do something you've been putting off for a while.

- ❖ Try a new recipe (or restaurant).

- ❖ Write a letter to someone special.

- ❖ Fix something that is broken.

- ❖ Tell someone a joke.

- ❖ Get a facial, a manicure or a massage (or all three!).

- ❖ Go for a walk for at least 20 minutes. Notice the colors, shapes, textures and sounds around you.

- ❖ Write yourself a love letter.

- ❖ Help someone who is worse off than you are.

- ❖ Have someone read you a story.

- ❖ Make a list of 10 things you do great!

- ❖ Make a list of 10 things you're grateful for.

- ❖ Give someone in your family a back rub or foot massage.

❖ Clean out a drawer.

❖ Play hide-and-seek with your family.

❖ Read or watch something really funny.

❖ Eat dinner by candlelight.

❖ Call someone you care about.

❖ Do something special for someone—anonymously!

❖ Look at your beautiful self in a mirror. Say "I love you" 10 times!

❖ Volunteer.

❖ Do something you used to love doing as a child, perhaps something that you haven't done since.

❖ Make music! Sing, play an instrument, drum on the kitchen counters. Make some noise.

❖ Do something kind for a stranger (or an animal).

❖ Create more space and simplicity in your life. Go through your attic, garage or closets. Find at least three things to give away to someone less fortunate.

❖ Buy a wonderful card for a special friend. Send it!

❖ Make your favorite meal or dessert.

❖ Listen to your favorite kind of music.

❖ Spend some time on a hobby you've been neglecting.

❖ Send your family to a movie and curl up on the couch with a great book or your favorite movie. (Absolutely *no* chores allowed.)

❖ Read something uplifting.

❖ Take a nap with your child.

❖ Buy yourself a little goodie or toy—just for you.

❖ Take a bath.

❖ Take a nap.

❖ Hug your child, your dog or your spouse (or even all three!).

PART VIII

Writing Your Own Lists

Things I've Said That I Want My Children to Remember Forever

❖ _____

_____

❖ _____

_____

❖ _____

_____

❖ _____

_____

❖ _____

_____

❖ _____

_____

❖ _____

_____

❖ _____

_____

❖ _____

_____

Things I Respect and Admire
About My Children

❖ _____
_____

❖ _____
_____

❖ _____
_____

❖ _____
_____

❖ _____
_____

❖ _____
_____

❖ _____
_____

❖ _____
_____

❖ _____
_____

Things About My Parenting That I'm Really Proud Of

❖ _____
_____

❖ _____
_____

❖ _____
_____

❖ _____
_____

❖ _____
_____

❖ _____
_____

❖ _____
_____

❖ _____
_____

❖ _____
_____

Things I Hope My Children Say About Me After I'm Gone

❖ _____

_____

❖ _____

_____

❖ _____

_____

❖ _____

_____

❖ _____

_____

❖ _____

_____

❖ _____

_____

❖ _____

_____

❖ _____

_____

Ways I've Shown Love
to My Children

❖ _____

_____

❖ _____

_____

❖ _____

_____

❖ _____

_____

❖ _____

_____

❖ _____

_____

❖ _____

_____

❖ _____

_____

❖ _____

_____

Things I've Done As Well As
My Own Parents Did
(in My Relationships with My Children)

❖ _____

_____

❖ _____

_____

❖ _____

_____

❖ _____

_____

❖ _____

_____

❖ _____

_____

❖ _____

_____

❖ _____

_____

Things I've Done Even
Better Than My Own Parents Did
(in My Relationships with My Children)

❖ _____

_____

❖ _____

_____

❖ _____

_____

❖ _____

_____

❖ _____

_____

❖ _____

_____

❖ _____

_____

❖ _____

_____

Things I Hope My Children Have Learned from Me

❖ _____

_____

❖ _____

_____

❖ _____

_____

❖ _____

_____

❖ _____

_____

❖ _____

_____

❖ _____

_____

❖ _____

_____

❖ _____

_____

Things I've Done or Said That I Hope My Children Can Forgive

❖ _____

_____

❖ _____

_____

❖ _____

_____

❖ _____

_____

❖ _____

_____

❖ _____

_____

❖ _____

_____

❖ _____

_____

❖ _____

_____

Things I Would Like to Change in My Relationships with My Children

❖ _____

_____

❖ _____

_____

❖ _____

_____

❖ _____

_____

❖ _____

_____

❖ _____

_____

❖ _____

_____

❖ _____

_____

❖ _____

_____

Things I'm Willing to Change in My Own Behavior

❖ _____
_____

❖ _____
_____

❖ _____
_____

❖ _____
_____

❖ _____
_____

❖ _____
_____

❖ _____
_____

❖ _____
_____

❖ _____
_____

Resources and Bibliography

▼

The hundreds of ideas in this book have been collected over the past decade or so from parents, educators, counselors and other adults in workshops and interviews; from books, articles, tapes and lectures; and from my own observations. Additionally, practically every list contains one or more ideas that were either suggested, demonstrated or validated by individuals whose names I do not know (or who wished to remain anonymous). In all other instances, I have attempted to acknowledge specific contributors for ideas they shared on particular topics. I have also included several references that were not used as resources for the ideas in this book, but that have similar or supporting information on relevant topics.

References that provided material for the lists have been marked with an asterisk.

Part I: Character Building

12 Ways to Be an Effective Mentor

Bluestein, Jane. *Mentors, Masters and Mrs. MacGregor: Stories of Teachers Making a Difference.* Deerfield Beach, Fla.: Health Communications, 1995.

——————. *Secrets of Successful Mentorship.* Albuquerque: ISS Publications, 1996.

12 Ways to Model Responsibility and Self-Discipline

*Algozzine, Bob. *Teacher's Little Book of Wisdom.* Merrillville, Ind.: ICS Books, 1995.

*Bluestein, Jane. "What's Wrong with I-Messages?" In *Book of Article Reprints.* Albuquerque: ISS Publications, 1995.

*McDaniel, Sandy Spurgeon. *Recipes from Parenting.* Newport Beach, Calif.: Spurgeon House Publications, 1990.

Moorman, Chick. *Talk Sense to Yourself: The Language of Personal Power.* Saginaw, Mich.: Personal Power Press, 1988.

9 Characteristics of Responsible, Self-Managing Children

*Bluestein, Jane, and Lynn Collins. *Parents in a Pressure Cooker.* Rosemont, N.J.: Modern Learning Press, 1989.

10 Ways to Encourage Responsibility, Independence and Self-Management

*Bluestein, Jane. *Proactive Parenting, Book 1: Characteristics of Great Parent-Child Relationships.* Albuquerque: ISS Publications, 1997.

*Bluestein, Jane, and Lynn Collins. *Parents in a Pressure Cooker.* Rosemont, N.J.: Modern Learning Press, 1989.

Cline, Foster, and Jim Fay. *Parenting with Love and Logic: Teaching Children Responsibility.* Colorado Springs, Colo.: NavPress, 1990.

Coloroso, Barbara. *Kids Are Worth It! Giving Your Child the Gift of Inner Discipline.* New York: William Morrow, 1994.

*Crary, Elizabeth. *Magic Tools for Raising Kids.* Seattle: Parenting Press, 1995.

——————. *Pick Up Your Socks . . . and Other Skills Growing Children Need!* Seattle: Parenting Press, 1990.

Dinkmeyer, Don, Sr., and Gary McKay. *Parenting Teenagers.* Circle Pines, Minn.: American Guidance Service, 1990.

——————. *The Parent's Handbook.* Circle Pines, Minn.: American Guidance Service, 1997.

——————. *Raising a Responsible Child: Practical Steps to Successful Family Relationships.* New York: Simon and Schuster, 1973.

Kvols, Kathryn. *Redirecting Children's Behavior.* Seattle: Parenting Press, 1997.

15 Characteristics of Children at Risk

Risk Check for Your Child [handout from Garfield Middle School, Albuquerque, New Mexico].

7 Characteristics of Families of Kids at Risk

*Freeman, Jodi. *How to Drug-Proof Kids.* Albuquerque: Think Shop, 1989.

*Risk Check for Your Child [handout from Garfield Middle School, Albuquerque, New Mexico].

10 Dangers of Encouraging Obedience and People-Pleasing

*Bluestein, Jane. Proactive Parenting, Book 2: Ten Common Parenting Mistakes—and What to Do Instead. Albuquerque: ISS Publications, 1997.

*Bluestein, Jane, and Lynn Collins. "Is Obedience Enough?" In Book of Article Reprints. Albuquerque: ISS Publications, 1995.

——————. Parents in a Pressure Cooker. Rosemont, N.J.: Modern Learning Press, 1989.

*Espeland, Pamela, and Rosemary Wallner. Making the Most of Today: Daily Readings for Young People on Self-Awareness, Creativity and Self-Esteem. Minneapolis: Free Spirit Publishing, 1991. [for quote by Bill Cosby on page 173].

16 Ways to Model Courtesy and 13 Ways to Model Respect

*Peggy Bielen, Deborah Critzer, Syndi Ecker, Julie Scurry West.

Baldrige, Letitia. More Than Manners: Raising Today's Kids to Have Kind Manners and Good Hearts. New York: Simon and Schuster, 1997.

19 Ways to Build Environmental Consciousness

*Patty Sheehan, Linda Sorenson.

*"Earth in Recovery." Families in Recovery, Nov.-Dec. 1990: 25.

Kohl, MaryAnn. Good Earth Art: Environmental Art for Kids. Bellingham, Wash.: Bright Ring Publishing, 1991.

17 Ways to Build Tolerance, Compassion and Global Consciousness

*Linda Sorenson.

Cole, Jim. *Filtering People.* Philadelphia: New Society Publishers, 1990.

Daleo, Morgan Simone. *Curriculum of Love: Cultivating the Spiritual Nature of Children.* Charlottesville, Va.: Grace Publishing, 1996.

Duvall, Lynn. *Respecting Our Differences: A Guide to Getting Along in a Changing World.* Minneapolis: Free Spirit Publishing, 1994.

Erlbach, Arlene. *The Families Book.* Minneapolis: Free Spirit Publishing, 1996.

Lalli, Judy. *Make Someone Smile and 40 More Ways to Be a Peaceful Person.* Minneapolis: Free Spirit Publishing, 1996.

Lewis, Barbara. *The Kid's Guide to Service Projects.* Minneapolis: Free Spirit Publishing, 1995.

——————. *The Kid's Guide to Social Action.* Minneapolis: Free Spirit Publishing, 1991.

Teaching Tolerance [a free, semi-annual magazine with ideas for teachers on promoting interracial and multicultural understanding; 400 Washington Ave., Montgomery, AL 36104; fax 334-264-3121].

15 Ways to Model and Teach Optimism

Espeland, Pamela, and Rosemary Wallner. *Making the Most of Today: Daily Readings for Young People on Self-Awareness, Creativity and Self-Esteem.* Minneapolis: Free Spirit Publishing, 1991.

Seligman, Martin E. P. *The Optimistic Child: A Proven Program to Safeguard Children Against Depression and Build Resilience.* New York: Houghton Mifflin, 1995.

8 Ways to Model and Teach Gratitude

*Loretta Maase, Patty Sheehan.

Daleo, Morgan Simone. *Curriculum of Love: Cultivating the Spiritual Nature of Children.* Charlottesville, Va.: Grace Publishing, 1996.

15 Ways to Model Self-Care

*Lynn Collins, Loretta Maase, Bob Moawad, Patty Sheehan, Bruce Williamson.

Adderholdt-Elliott, Miriam. *Perfectionism: What's Bad About Being Too Good?* Minneapolis: Free Spirit Publishing, 1987.

Burns, David D. *The Feeling Good Handbook.* New York: Plume, 1980.

Cole, Jim. *Thwarting Anger: A View of How We Keep Anger Alive.* Novato, Calif.: Growing Images, 1985.

*Guenther, Nella Bunny. "Parenting Your Inner Child." *Families in Recovery,* Sept.-Oct. 1990, 19-20.

W., Lynn, ed. *Mending Ourselves: Expressions of Healing and Self-Integration.* Cincinnati, Many Voices Press, 1993.

Young, Jeffrey E., and Janet S. Klosko. *Reinventing Your Life.* New York: Dutton, 1993.

Related Topics

Catalfo, Phil. *Raising Spiritual Children in a Material World: Introducing Spirituality into Family Life.* New York: Berkeley Books, 1997.

Cline, Foster, and Jim Fay. *Parenting with Love and Logic: Teaching Children Responsibility.* Colorado Springs, Colo.: Piñon Press, 1990.

Coles, Robert. *The Moral Intelligence of Children.* New York: Random House, 1997.

Eyre, Linda, and Richard Eyre. *Teaching Your Children Sensitivity.* New York: Simon and Schuster, 1987.

——————. *Teaching Your Children Values.* New York: Simon and Schuster, 1993.

Glenn, H. Stephen, and Jane Nelsen. *Raising Self-Reliant Children in a Self-Indulgent World: Seven Building Blocks for Developing Capable Young People.* Rocklin, Calif.: Prima Publishing, 1988.

Popkin, Michael. *Active Parenting: Teaching Cooperation, Courage and Responsibility.* San Francisco: HarperSanFrancisco, 1987.

Popov, Linda Kavelin. *The Family Virtues Guide.* New York: A Plume Book, 1997.

Shapiro, Lawrence E. *How to Raise a Child with a High E.Q. (Emotional Quotient): A Parent's Guide to Emotional Intelligence.* New York: HarperCollins, 1997.

Part II: Wheeling and Dealing: Motivation, Cooperation and Avoiding Power Struggles

14 Ways to Create a Win-Win Home Environment

*Bluestein, Jane. *No-Lose Parenting.* Albuquerque: ISS Publications, 1996.

6 Ways to Accommodate Your Child's Need for Control— Without Losing Control Yourself!

*Bluestein, Jane. *Parents, Teens and Boundaries.* Deerfield Beach, Fla.: Health Communications, 1993.

*Bluestein, Jane, and Lynn Collins. *Parents in a Pressure Cooker.* Rosemont, N.J.: Modern Learning Press, 1989.

*Crary, Elizabeth. *Love and Limits: Guidance Tools for Creative Parenting.* Seattle: Parenting Press, 1994.

——————. *Magic Tools for Raising Kids.* Seattle: Parenting Press, 1995.

10 Reasons to Offer Choices or Negotiate Options with Your Child

*Bluestein, Jane. *Parents, Teens and Boundaries.* Deerfield Beach, Fla.: Health Communications, 1993.

*Bluestein, Jane, and Lynn Collins. *Parents in a Pressure Cooker.* Rosemont, N.J.: Modern Learning Press, 1989.

*Crary, Elizabeth. *Magic Tools for Raising Kids.* Seattle: Parenting Press, 1995.

11 Reasons to Use Boundaries *and* 9 Things to Remember When Setting a Boundary

*Bluestein, Jane. *Following Through.* Albuquerque: ISS Publications, 1996.

——————. *Parents, Kids and Boundaries.* Albuquerque: ISS Publications, 1997. Audiocassette.

——————. *Parents, Teens and Boundaries.* Deerfield Beach, Fla.: Health Communications, 1993.

————————. *21st Century Discipline: Teaching Students Responsibility and Self-Control* 2nd ed. Albuquerque: ISS Publications, 1997.

Cole, Jim. *The Helpers: A View of Our Helpfulness.* Novato, Calif.: Growing Images, 1990.

MacKenzie, Robert J. *Setting Limits: How to Raise Responsible, Independent Children by Providing Reasonable Boundaries.* Rocklin, Calif.: Prima Publishing, 1993.

18 Things to Remember About Motivation

*Bluestein, Jane. *Parents, Teens and Boundaries.* Deerfield Beach, Fla.: Health Communications, 1993.

————————. *Proactive Parenting, Book 4: Motivation and Cooperation.* Albuquerque: ISS Publications, 1997.

*McDaniel, Sandy Spurgeon. *Recipes from Parenting.* Newport Beach, Calif.: Spurgeon House Publications, 1990.

Related Topics

Ames, Louise Bates. *Raising Good Kids: A Developmental Approach to Discipline.* Rosemont, N.J.: Modern Learning Press, 1992.

Coletta, Anthony. *What's Best for Kids: A Guide to Developmentally Appropriate Practices for Teachers and Parents of Children Age 4–8.* Rosemont, N.J.: Modern Learning Press, 1991.

Crary, Elizabeth. *Help! The Kids Are at It Again: Using Kids' Quarrels to Teach "People Skills."* Seattle: Parenting Press, 1997.

————————. *Without Spanking or Spoiling: A Practical Approach to Toddler and Preschool Guidance.* Seattle: Parenting Press, 1993.

Faber, Adele, and Elaine Mazlish. *How to Talk So Kids Will Listen and Listen So Kids Will Talk.* New York: Avon Books, 1980.

Nelsen, Jane. *Positive Discipline.* New York: Ballantine, 1996.

Whitham, Cynthia. *The Answer Is No: Saying It and Sticking to It.* Los Angeles: Perspective Publishing, 1994.

—————. *Win the Whining War and Other Skirmishes: A Family Peace Plan.* Los Angeles: Perspective Publishing, 1995.

Part III: Relationship Building and Getting Along (Emotional Safety)

9 Ways to Create Emotional Safety in Your Relationship with Your Child

*Bluestein, Jane. *Proactive Parenting, Book 1: Characteristics of Great Parent-Child Relationships.* Albuquerque: ISS Publications, 1997.

—————. "What's Wrong with I-Messages?" In *Book of Article Reprints.* Albuquerque: ISS Publications, 1995.

*Ford, Judy. *Wonderful Ways to Love a Child.* Berkeley, Calif.: Conari Press, 1995.

*McDaniel, Sandy Spurgeon. *Recipes from Parenting.* Newport Beach, Calif.: Spurgeon House Publications, 1990.

12 Reasons a Child May Want to Join a Gang

*Dr. Louis Gonzales.

8 Things to Remember About Saying "I Love You"

*Lynn Collins, Andy Quiñones.

*Bluestein, Jane. "Saying 'I Love You.'" In *Book of Article Reprints.* Albuquerque: ISS Publications, 1995.

12 Ways to Increase Positivity in Your Interactions

*Kathy Hayes.

*Bluestein, Jane. *Positively Positive!* Albuquerque: ISS Publications, 1996.

*Crary, Elizabeth. *Magic Tools for Raising Kids.* Seattle: Parenting Press, 1995.

Espeland, Pamela, and Rosemary Wallner. *Making the Most of Today: Daily Readings for Young People on Self-Awareness, Creativity and Self-Esteem.* Minneapolis: Free Spirit Publishing, 1991.

Related Topics

*Bluestein, Jane. *Proactive Parenting, Book 2: Ten Common Parenting Mistakes—and What to Do Instead.* Albuquerque: ISS Publications, 1997.

Fay, Jim. *Helicopters, Drill Sergeants and Consultants: Parenting Styles and the Messages They Send.* Golden, Colo.: The Love and Logic Press, 1994.

Marston, Stephanie. *The Magic of Encouragement: Nurturing Your Child's Self-Esteem.* New York: Pocket Books, 1990.

Prather, Hugh, and Gayle Prather. *Spiritual Parenting: A Guide to Understanding and Nurturing the Heart of Your Child.* New York: Three Rivers Press, 1996.

Rathbon, Natalie. *The Unmotivated Child.* New York: Fireside Books, 1996.

Part IV: Skill Building, Learning and Personal Growth

14 Ways to Encourage a Lifelong Love of Learning

Dryden, Gordon, and Jeannette Vos. *The Learning Revolution.* Carson, Calif.: Jalmar Press, 1994.

Hunt, D. Trinidad. *Learning to Learn: Maximizing Your Performance Potential.* Kaneohe, Hawaii: Elan Enterprises, 1991.

Markova, Dawna. *How Your Child Is Smart.* Berkeley, Calif.: Conari Press, 1992.

——————. *The Open Mind.* Berkeley, Calif.: Conari Press, 1996.

McCutcheon, Randall. *Can You Find It? Library Scavenger Hunts to Sharpen Your Research Skills.* Minneapolis: Free Spirit Publishing, 1991.

*Ohme, Herman. *Learn How to Learn Study Skills.* Palo Alto, Calif.: California Education Plan, 1994.

——————. *101 Ways for Parents to Motivate Students.* Palo Alto, Calif.: California Education Plan, 1986.

Vitale, Barbara Meister. *Free Flight: Celebrating Your Right Brain.* Carson, Calif.: Jalmar Press, 1986.

——————. *Unicorns Are Real: A Right-Brained Approach to Learning.* Carson, Calif.: Jal-Mar Press, 1982.

Waas, Lane Longino. *Imagine That! Getting Smarter Through Imagery Practice.* Carson, Calif.: Jalmar Press, 1991.

*Williamson, Bruce. "Wondering Around." *Families in Recovery,* Sept.-Oct. 1990, 9.

15 Ways to Accommodate Your Child's Success Needs *and* 8 Things to Do When Your Child Makes a Mistake

*Lynn Collins, Gregg Edward, Sandi Redenbach.

Adderholdt-Elliott, Miriam, *Perfectionism: What's Bad About Being Too Good?* Minneapolis: Free Spirit Publishing, 1987.

Ames, Louise Bates. *What Do They Mean I'm Difficult?* Rosemont, N.J.: Modern Learning Press, 1986.

Barrett, Susan L. *It's All in Your Head: A Guide to Understanding Your Brain and Boosting Brain Power.* Minneapolis: Free Spirit Publishing, 1992.

Benson, Peter L., Judy Galbraith, and Pamela Espeland. *What Kids Need to Succeed: Proven, Practical Ways to Raise Good Kids.* Minneapolis: Free Spirit Publishing, 1995.

*Crary, Elizabeth. *Love and Limits: Guidance Tools for Creative Parenting.* Seattle: Parenting Press, 1994.

*Racosky, Richard. *Dreams + Action = Reality.* Boulder, Colo.: ActionGraphics Publishing, 1996.

13 Ways to Build Decision-Making Skills

*Bluestein, Jane, and Lynn Collins. *Parents in a Pressure Cooker.* Rosemont, N.J.: Modern Learning Press, 1989.

Crary, Elizabeth. *Kids Can Cooperate: A Practical Guide to Teaching Problem Solving.* Seattle: Parenting Press, 1984.

——————. *Problem Solving Books for Children Series.* Volumes include: *I Can't Wait; I Want to Play; I Want It; I'm Lost; Mommy Don't Go;* and *My Name Is Not Dummy.* Seattle: Parenting Press, 1996.

Tracy, Louise Felton. *Grounded for Life: Stop Blowing Your Fuse and Start Communicating with Your Teenager.* Seattle: Parenting Press, 1994.

19 Ways to Build Thinking Skills

*Lisa Cramer, Deborah Critzer, Tami Gerrard, Dr. Karen Sides Gonzales.

*Halene Weaver, for teaching me more about the use of collections for concept and vocabulary development.

*Bluestein, Jane. *Proactive Parenting, Book 3: Building Commitment and Decision-Making Skills.* Albuquerque: ISS Publications, 1997.

Dexter, Sandi. *Joyful Play with Toddlers.* Seattle: Parenting Press, 1995.

Robinson, Jonathan. *The Little Book of Big Questions.* Berkeley, Calif.: Conari Press, 1995.

Steelsmith, Shari. *Peekaboo and Other Games to Play with Your Baby.* Seattle: Parenting Press, 1995.

23 Ways to Encourage Creativity and Imagination

*Patty Sheehan.

Cameron, Julia. *The Artist's Way.* New York: Jeremy Tarcher/Putnam, 1992.

Dahlstrom, Lorraine M. *Doing the Days: A Year's Worth of Creative Journaling, Drawing, Listening, Reading, Thinking, Arts and Crafts Activities for Children Ages 8–12.* Minneapolis: Free Spirit Publishing, 1994.

*Ford, Judy. *Wonderful Ways to Love a Child.* Berkeley, Calif.: Conari Press, 1995.

Kohl, MaryAnn. *Mudworks: Creative Clay, Dough, and Modeling Experiences.* Bellingham, Wash.: Bright Ring Publishing, 1989.

——————. *Scribble Arts: Independent Creative Art Experiences for Children.* Bellingham, Wash.: Bright Ring Publishing, 1994.

10 Ways to Encourage an Appreciation for the Arts

*Sylvana Clark, MaryAnn Kohl, Linda Sorenson.

31 Ways to Develop Literacy and a Love of Reading

*Sylvana Clark, Deborah Critzer, MaryAnn Kohl, Linda Sorenson.

Dahlstrom, Lorraine M. *Doing the Days: A Year's Worth of Creative Journaling, Drawing, Listening, Reading, Thinking, Arts and Crafts Activities for Children Ages 8–12.* Minneapolis: Free Spirit Publishing, 1994.

——————. *Writing Down the Days: 365 Creative Journaling Ideas for Young People.* Minneapolis: Free Spirit Publishing, 1990.

Daleo, Morgan Simone. *The Book of Dreams and Visions: Creative Journaling with Night Dreams and Day Dreams for Understanding and Inspiration.* Charlottesville, Va.: Grace Publishing, 1996.

Reading Is Fundamental [write: RIF, Department WB, P.O. Box 23444, Washington, D.C. 20026. Web site: http://www.si.edu/rif.]

*Spencer, Gwynne. "Easy Twists Can Perk Up Reading Time." *Albuquerque Tribune,* 14 May 1997.

*Williamson, Bruce. "Re-Storying Yourself." *Families in Recovery,* Nov.-Dec. 1990, 8.

9 Ways to Minimize Problems with Homework

*Deborah Critzer, Julie Scurry West.

*Ohme, Herman. *101 Ways for Parents to Motivate Students.* Palo Alto, Calif.: California Education Plan, 1986.

*Radencich, Marguerite C., and Jeanne S. Schumm. *How to Help Your Child with Homework.* Minneapolis: Free Spirit Publishing, 1997.

Romain, Trevor. *How to Do Homework Without Throwing Up.* Minneapolis, Free Spirit Publishing, 1997.

*Whitham, Cynthia. *The Answer Is No: Saying It and Sticking to It.* Los Angeles: Perspective Publishing, 1994.

17 Ways to Build Positive Relationships with Your Child's Teachers

*Bluestein, Jane. "I'm Calling Your Mother: Boundary Setting with Your Child's Teachers." In *Book of Article Reprints.* Albuquerque: ISS Publications, 1995.

——————. *Proactive Parenting, Book 5: Building School Success.* Albuquerque: ISS Publications, 1997.

*Ohme, Herman. *101 Ways for Parents to Motivate Students.* Palo Alto, Calif.: California Education Plan, 1986.

Related Topics

Bosch, Carl W. *Making the Grade.* Seattle: Parenting Press, 1991.

Chen, Milton. *The Smart Parent's Guide to Kids' TV.* San Francisco, Calif.: KQED Books, 1994.

Grant, Jim. *I Hate School.* Rosemont, N.J.: Modern Learning Press, 1994.

Martin, Michael, and Cynthia Waltman-Greenwood, eds. *Solve Your Child's School-Related Problems.* National Association of School Psychologists. New York: HarperPerennial, 1995.

McCutcheon, Randall. *Get Off My Brain: A Survival Guide for Lazy Students.* Minneapolis: Free Spirit Publishing, 1985.

Tracy, Louise Felton. *Grounded for Life: Stop Blowing Your Fuse and Start Communicating with Your Teenager.* Seattle: Parenting Press, 1994.

Vail, Priscilla. *About Dyslexia: Unraveling the Myth.* Rosemont, N.J.: Modern Learning Press, 1990.

Part V: Problem Solving and Prevention

6 Reasons *Not* to Give Your Child Advice

*Algozzine, Bob. *Teacher's Little Book of Wisdom.* Merrillville, Ind.: ICS Books, 1995.

11 Ways to Encourage Cooperation with Chores

*Lynn Collins, MaryAnn Kohl, Loretta Maase.

Job List: A New Child Organizer [weekly chore chart published by Character Builders, Winter Park, Fla., phone: 407-677-7171].

Kids Work [a weekly picture chore chart for prereaders published by Sugar Sign Press, Greensboro N.C., phone: 919-273-9838].

*Stockham, Karen. "Master Your Disaster." *Families in Recovery* 2, no. 1 (1991: 39-141.)

3 Ways to Deal with a Messy Room

*Jo Lynne Jones, MaryAnn Kohl.

*Stockham, Karen. "Master Your Disaster." *Families in Recovery* 2, no. 1 (1991: 3-4.)

12 Ways to Avoid Problems at Bedtime

*Bluestein, Jane. "Bedtime Without a Battle." In *Book of Article Reprints.* Albuquerque: ISS Publications, 1995.

Huntley, Rebecca. *The Sleep Book for Tired Parents: Help for Solving Children's Sleep Problems.* Seattle: Parenting Press, 1991.

Mindell, Jodi A. *Sleeping Through the Night: How Infants, Toddlers and Their Parents Can Get a Good Night's Sleep.* New York: HarperPerennial, 1997.

14 Ways to Help Your Child Deal with Monsters in the Closet

*Loretta Maase, Mark and Teresa Smith.

*Joslin, Karen Renshaw. "Fear of Dark." In *Positive Parenting from A to Z.* New York: Fawcett Columbine, 1994.

10 Things to Remember About Potty Training Your Child

*Deborah Critzer, Karen Sides Gonzales, Julie Scurry West.

*Eisenberg, Arlene, Heidi E. Murkoff, and Sandee E., Hathaway. "Sitting Pretty: What You Gotta Do When They Gotta Go." *Parent's Digest,* Fall/Winter 1995: 31-33.

*Faull, Jan. *Mommy, I Have to Go Potty.* Hemet, Calif.: Raefield-Roberts *and* Seattle: Parenting Press, 1996.

Lansky, Vicki. *Koko Bear's New Potty.* Minnetonka, Minn.: Book Peddlers, 1997.

16 Ways to Avoid Conflicts over Food

*Carol Bell, Lynn Cramer, Loretta Maase, Brooke Richards.

Folkers, Gladys, and Jeanne Englemann. *Taking Charge of My Mind and Body: A Girls' Guide to Outsmarting Alcohol, Drug, Smoking and Eating Problems.* Minneapolis: Free Spirit Publishing, 1997.

*Hirschmann, Jane R., and Lela Zaphiropoulos. *Preventing Childhood Eating Problems.* Carlsbad, Calif.: Gurze Books, 1993.

*Joslin, Karen Renshaw. *Positive Parenting from A to Z.* New York: Fawcett Columbine, 1994.

*Wilkes, Norma Jean. "Mealtimes Your Children Can Swallow." *Families in Recovery,* Sept.-Oct. 1990: 12-13, 23.

10 Ways to Minimize or Avoid Problems at the Grocery Store

*Carol Bell, Lisa Cramer, Kathryn Kvols, Loretta Maase.

11 Ways to Avoid Problems over Money or Buying

*Peggy Bielen, Judy Lawrence, Kathy Morey.

Bodnar, Janet. *Kiplinger's Money Smart Kids (and Parent's, Too!).* Washington, D.C.: Kiplinger Books, 1993.

Gallagher, Trisha. *Raising Happy Kids on a Reasonable Budget.* Cincinnati: Better Way Books, 1993.

Godfrey, Neale S., and Carolina Edwards. *Money Doesn't Grow on Trees: A Parent's Guide to Raising Financially Responsible Children.* New York: Fireside Books, 1994.

Modu, Emmanuel. *The Lemonade Stand: A Guide to Encouraging the Entrepreneur in Your Child.* Newark, N.J.: Gateway Publishers, 1996.

Searls, Michael J. *Kids and Money: A Hands-On Parent's Guide to Teach Children About Successful Money Management and Business Basics.* Englewood, Colo.: World of Money Books, 1996.

14 Ways to Encourage Positive Choices for Good Health and Safety

*Lisa Cramer, Karen Sides Gonzales, Julie Scurry West.

Behan, Eileen. *Meals That Heal for Babies, Toddlers and Children.* New York: Pocket Books, 1996.

Bennett, Steve, and Ruth Bennett. *365 Outdoor Activities You Can Do with Your Child.* Holbrook, Mass.: Adams Publishing, 1993.

——————. *365 TV-Free Activities You Can Do with Your Child.* Holbrook, Mass.: Adams Publishing, 1991.

Boelts, Maribeth, and Darwin Boelts. *Kids to the Rescue! First Aid Techniques for Kids.* Seattle: Parenting Press, 1992.

*Fastle, Donna. "Harnessing Halloween Horrors." *Families in Recovery,* Sept.-Oct. 1990: 5-6.

*Freeman, Lory. *It's My Body.* Seattle: Parenting Press, 1982.

*——————. *Loving Touches.* Seattle: Parenting Press, 1986.

*Hammerseng, Kathryn M. *Telling Isn't Tattling.* Seattle: Parenting Press, 1995.

Johnson, Karen. *The Trouble with Secrets.* Seattle: Parenting Press, 1986.

Kehoe, Patricia. *Something Happened and I'm Scared to Tell: A Book for Young Victims of Abuse.* Seattle: Parenting Press, 1987.

Lansky, Vicki. *Baby Proofing Basic.* Minnetonka, Minn.: Book Peddlers, 1991.

Saunders, Carol Silverman. *Safe at School: Awareness and Action for Parents of Kids Grades K–12*. Minneapolis: Free Spirit Publishing, 1994.

11 Ways to Create Success with Your Baby-Sitter

Beecham, Jahnna, and Malcolm Hillgartner. *The Babysitter's Club Guide to Babysitting*. New York: Scholastic, 1993.

*Joslin, Karen Renshaw. *Positive Parenting from A to Z*. New York: Fawcett Columbine, 1994.

15 Ways to Minimize Conflicts on Car Trips

Barry, Sheila Anne. *The World's Best Travel Games*. New York: Sterling Publishing, 1987.

*Gerrard, Tami. "Are We There Yet?" *Families in Recovery* 2, no. 3 (1991: 3-4.)

Kowitt, Holly. *Road Trip: A Travel Activity Book*. New York: Scholastic, 1994.

Kuch, Kayte. *50 Nifty: More Travel Games*. Los Angeles: Lowell House Juvenile, 1995.

Paulsen, Larry. *Glove Compartment Games*. Palo Alto, Calif.: Klutz (Wood-Howard Products), 1997.

Taylor, Kevin, and Joan Taylor. *50 Nifty Travel Games*. Los Angeles: Lowell House Juvenile, 1997.

15 Ways to Drug-Proof Your Child

*Deborah Critzer, Julie Scurry West.

Carbone, Elisa. *Corey's Story: Her Family's Secret*. Burlington, Vt.: Waterfront Books, 1997.

*Freeman, Jodi. *How to Drug-Proof Kids.* Albuquerque: Think Shop, 1989.

Folkers, Gladys, and Jeanne Englemann. *Taking Charge of My Mind and Body: A Girls' Guide to Outsmarting Alcohol, Drug, Smoking and Eating Problems.* Minneapolis: Free Spirit Publishing, 1997.

Hall, Lindsey, and Leigh Cohn. *Dear Kids of Alcoholics.* Carlsbad, Calif.: Gürze Books, 1988.

Johnson, Kendall. *Turning Yourself Around: Self-Help for Troubled Teens.* Alameda, Calif.: Hunter House, 1992.

Laik, Judy. *Under Whose Influence.* Seattle: Parenting Press, 1994.

Levenson, Nancy, and Joanne Rocklin. *Feeling Great: Reaching out to Life, Reaching in to Yourself—Without Drugs.* Alameda, Calif.: Hunter House, 1992.

Related Topics

Faber, Adele, and Elaine Mazlish. *Siblings Without Rivalry.* New York: Avon Books, 1987.

Part VI: Dealing with Feelings (Supportiveness)

5 Reasons to Help Your Children Learn to Express Their Feelings in Healthy, Nondestructive Ways *and* 17 Ways to Make It Safe for Your Child to Have and Express Feelings

*Bluestein, Jane. "Being a Supportive Listener." In *Book of Article Reprints* Albuquerque: ISS Publications, 1995.

*————. "Dealing with Feelings." Albuquerque: ISS Publications, 1997. Audiocassette.

*————————. *Parents, Teens and Boundaries.* Deerfield Beach, Fla.: Health Communications, 1993.

*Collins, Lynn. "Help! My Child's Having a Feeling." *Families in Recovery* 2, no. 2 (1991: 8-9.)

*Crary, Elizabeth. *Love and Limits: Guidance Tools for Creative Parenting.* Seattle: Parenting Press, 1994.

Elchoness, Monte. *Why Do Kids Need Feelings? A Guide to Healthy Emotions.* Ventura, Calif.: Monroe Press, 1992.

9 Characteristics of Good Listeners

*Bluestein, Jane. "Being a Supportive Listener." *Book of Article Reprints.* Albuquerque: ISS Publications, 1995.

Remen, Rachel Naomi. "Listening, A Powerful Tool for Healing." *Science of Mind* 70, no. 7 (July 1997: 18.)

14 Ways to Respect Your Child's Reality

*Deborah Critzer, Dr. Kathy Hayes, Maurine Renville, Julie Scurry West.

*Algozzine, Bob. *Teacher's Little Book of Wisdom,* Merrillville, Ind.: ICS Books, 1995.

*Ford, Judy. *Wonderful Ways to Love a Teen . . . Even When It Seems Impossible.* Berkeley, Calif.: Conari Press, 1996.

16 Things You Can Suggest to Help Your Child Let Out Anger Nondestructively

*Crary, Elizabeth. *I'm Furious.* Seattle: Parenting Press, 1994.

*————————. *I'm Mad.* Seattle: Parenting Press, 1994.

12 Things *Never* to Say When Your Child's Feelings Have Been Hurt

*Bluestein, Jane. "Being a Supportive Listener." In *Book of Article Reprints.* Albuquerque: ISS Publications, 1995.

13 Ways to Help Your Child Deal with Death or Loss

*Deborah Critzer, Loretta Maase, Julie Scurry West.

Gootman, Marilyn E. *When a Friend Dies.* Minneapolis: Free Spirit Publishing, 1994.

*Grossman, Rabbi Rafael, and Anna Olswanger. "A Very Special Explanation." *Parenting New Mexico,* March 1996: 12-13.

*Kroen, William C. *Helping Children Cope with the Loss of a Loved One: A Guide for Grownups.* Minneapolis: Free Spirit Publishing, 1996. [For the quote on commemorating a loved one, see page 77].

Maple, Marilyn. *On the Wings of a Butterfly: A Story About Life and Death.* Seattle: Parenting Press, 1992.

17 Ways to Help Your Children Survive Your Divorce

*Diane Clements, Heather Clements, Dr. Kathy Hayes, Dave Hinckley, Bob Hoekstra, Samantha Hoekstra, Judy Lawrence, Debbie Madison, Evelyn Mercur, S. J. Sanchez, Dr. Bettie B. Youngs.

Anderson, Joan. *The Single Mother's Book: A Practical Guide to Managing Your Children, Career, Home, Finances and Everything Else.* Atlanta: Peachtree Publishers, 1990.

Bienenfeld, Florence. *Helping Your Child Succeed After Divorce.* Alameda, Calif.: Hunter House Publishing, 1987.

Children's Rights Council. *The Best Parent Is Both Parents.* Washington, D.C.

Fassler, David, Michele Lash, and Sally Ives. *Changing Families: An Interactive Guide for Kids and Grownups.* Burlington, Vt.: Waterfront Books, 1988.

Ives, Sally B., David Fassler, and Michele Lash. *The Divorce Workbook: An Interactive Guide for Kids and Grownups.* Burlington, Vt.: Waterfront Books, 1985.

Lash, Michele, Sally Ives Loughridge, and David Fassler. *My Kind of Family: A Book for Kids from Single-Parent Homes.* Burlington, Vt.: Waterfront Books, 1990.

My Two Homes [divorce calendar for kids to keep track of custody and home-sharing schedules, transitions, holidays, birthdays and other important events, published by Ladybug Press, Albuquerque, N.M., 1-800-244-1761].

Related Topics

*Bluestein, Jane. *Proactive Parenting, Book 6: Feelings and Problem Solving.* Albuquerque: ISS Publications, 1997.

Cecil, Nancy Lee. *Raising Peaceful Children in a Violent World.* San Diego: Lura Media, 1995.

*Crary, Elizabeth. *Dealing with Feelings Series.* Volumes include: *I'm Mad; I'm Sad; I'm Furious; I'm Excited; I'm Scared;* and *I'm Proud.* Dealing with Feelings. Seattle: Parenting Press, Inc., 1994.

Kaufman, Gershen, and Lev Raphael. *Stick Up for Yourself: Every Kid's Guide to Personal Power and Positive Self-Esteem.* Minneapolis: Free Spirit Publishing, 1990.

Payne, Lauren Murphy. *Just Because I Am: A Child's Book of Affirmation.* Minneapolis: Free Spirit Publishing, 1994.

——————. *We Can Get Along: A Child's Book of Choices.* Minneapolis: Free Spirit Publishing, 1997.

Part VII: Healthy Parenting
(Personal Issues and Self-Care)

14 Ways to Become a More Conscious Parent

*Williamson, Bruce. "Wondering Around." *Families in Recovery,* Sept.-Oct. 1990: 9.

9 Ways to Be More Proactive

*Bluestein, Jane. *Proactivity—Thinking Ahead!* Albuquerque: ISS Publications, 1996.

*Crary, Elizabeth. *Magic Tools for Raising Kids.* Seattle: Parenting Press, 1995.

10 Ways to Avoid Getting Hooked by Your Child's Misbehavior *and* 13 Arguments for *Not* Hitting Your Child

*McDaniel, Sandy Spurgeon. *Recipes from Parenting.* Newport Beach, Calif.: Spurgeon House Publications, 1990.

Tracy, Louise Felton. *Grounded for Life: Stop Blowing Your Fuse and Start Communicating with Your Teenager.* Seattle: Parenting Press, 1994.

9 Things You Can Say to Detach from Unsolicited Advice or Criticism About Your Parenting Skills

*Special thanks to Peggy Bielen for introducing me to this technique.

*Hawkins, Rev. Norma. "Daily Guides to Richer Living." *Science of Mind* 70, no. 5 (May 1997).

10 Things to Remember About Changing Family Dynamics

Chernofsky, Barbara, and Diane Gage. *Change Your Child's Behavior by Changing Yours: 13 New Tricks to Get Kids to Cooperate.* New York: Random House, 1996.

Faber, Adele, and Elaine Mazlish. *Liberated Parents, Liberated Children: A Guide to a Happier Family.* New York: Avon Books, 1990.

Fishel, Elizabeth. *I Swore I'd Never Do That! Recognizing Family Patterns and Making Wise Parenting Choices.* Berkeley, Calif.: Conari Press, 1994.

*McDaniel, Sandy Spurgeon. *Recipes from Parenting.* Newport Beach, Calif.: Spurgeon House Publications, 1990.

Nelsen, Jane, Ricki Intner, and Lynn Lott. *Clean and Sober Parenting: A Guide to Help Recovering Parents Rebuild Trust, Create Structure, Improve Communications, Learn Parenting Skills and Give Up Guilt and Shame.* Rocklin, Calif.: Prima Publishing, 1992.

Tracy, Louise Felton. *Grounded for Life: Stop Blowing Your Fuse and Start Communicating with Your Teenager.* Seattle: Parenting Press, 1994.

10 Ways to Respect Your Parents as Grandparents

*Dudley, Mary. "You *Can* Go Home Again." *Families in Recovery* 2, no. 3 (1991): 14-15.

Erlbach, Arlene. *The Families Book*. Minneapolis: Free Spirit Publishing, 1996.

26 of the Best Things About Having Two-Year-Olds in Families

*Louise Ellenberger, Barb Fischer, David Friedli, Dr. Kathy Hayes, Dave Hinckley, Jo Lynne Jones, Kathryn Kvols, Sr. Mary Alyce Lach, Beth K. Lefevre, Sandi Redenbach, Brooke Richards, Tasneem Virani, Karen Wilkins, Dr. Bettie B. Youngs.

18 of the Best Things About Having a Teenager in the Family

*Louise Ellenberger, David Friedli, Dr. Kathy Hayes, Dave Hinckley, Kathryn Kvols, Beth K. Lefevre, Andy Quiñones, Sandi Redenbach, Brooke Richards, Tasneem Virani, Karen Wilkins, Dr. Bettie B. Youngs.

*Bluestein, Jane. *Parents, Teens and Boundaries*. Deerfield Beach, Fla.: Health Communications, 1993.

Craig, Judy. *You're Grounded 'Til You're Thirty*. New York: William Morrow, 1996.

Dinkmeyer, Don, Sr., and Gary McKay. *Parenting Teenagers*. Circle Pines, Minn.: American Guidance Service, Inc., 1990.

*Ford, Judy. *Wonderful Ways to Love a Teen . . . Even When It Seems Impossible*. Berkeley, Calif.: Conari Press, 1996.

Gardner, James E. *The Turbulent Teens*. Los Angeles: Sorrento Press, 1983.

Joslin, Karen Renshaw, and Mary Bunting Decher. *Positive Parenting Your Teens: The A-Z Book of Sound Advice and Practical Solutions*. New York: Fawcett Columbine, 1997.

Nelsen, Jane, and Lynn Lott. *Positive Discipline for Teenagers: Resolving Conflict with Your Teenage Son or Daughter.* Rocklin, Calif.: Prima Publishing, 1994.

Packer, Alex J. *Bringing Up Parents.* Minneapolis: Free Spirit Publishing, 1992.

Youngs, Bettie B. *Safeguarding Your Teenager from the Dragons of Life: A Guide to the Adolescent Years.* Deerfield Beach, Fla.: Health Communications, 1993.

10 Ways to Make More Time for Your Child

*Special thanks to Lisa Cramer for her "just-you-two day" idea.

*Karen Sides Gonzales, Julie Scurry West.

6 Ways to Take More Time for Yourself

*Bluestein, Jane. "Not Now! When You Need Space and Your Children Need You." In *Book of Article Reprints.* Albuquerque: ISS Publications, 1995.

Willis, Kay, and Maryann Brinley. *Are We Having Fun Yet?* New York: Warner Books, 1997.

36 Things You Can Do to Feel Great!

*Bruce Williamson.

*"Feel Good Calendar." *Families in Recovery,* Sept.-Oct. 1990: 16.

Levine, Arlene Gay. *39 Ways to Open Your Heart.* Berkeley, Calif.: Conari Press, 1996.

Schriner, Christian. *Feel Better Now: 30 Ways to Handle Frustration in Three Minutes or Less.* Carson, Calif.: Jalmar Press, 1990.

Related Topics

Adderholdt-Elliott, Miriam. *Perfectionism: What's Bad About Being Too Good?* Minneapolis: Free Spirit Publishing, 1987.

Brondino, Jeanne, et al. *Raising Each Other: A Book for Teens and Parents.* Alameda, Calif.: Hunter House, 1988.

Glennon, Will. *Fathering: Strengthening Connection with Your Children No Matter Where You Are.* Berkeley, Calif.: Conari Press, 1995.

Pillsbury, Linda Goodman. *Survival Tips for Working Moms.* Los Angeles: Perspective Publishing, 1994.

Other Books for Parents and Families

Branden, Nathaniel. *The Art of Living Consciously: The Power and Awareness to Transform Everyday Life.* New York: Simon & Schuster, 1997.

——————. *The Six Pillars of Self-Esteem.* New York: Bantam, 1994.

Brazelton, T. Berry. *Touchpoints: The Essential Reference: Your Child's Emotional and Behavioral Development.* Reading, Mass.: Addison-Wesley Publishing, 1992.

Coloroso, Barbara. *Kids Are Worth It! Giving Your Child the Gift of Inner Discipline.* New York: William Morrow, Inc., 1994.

Conner, Bobbi. *The Parent's Journal Guide to Raising Great Kids.* New York: Bantam Books, 1997.

Frankel, Fred. *Good Friends Are Hard to Find: Help Your Child Find, Make and Keep Friends.* Los Angeles: Perspective Publishing, 1996.

Grant, Jim. *Childhood Should Be a Precious Time: Anthology of Poems.* Rosemont, N.J.: Modern Learning Press, 1989.

Lindsay, Jeanne Warren. *Do I Have a Daddy? A Story About a Single-Parent Child.* Buena Park, Calif.: Morning Glory Press, 1991.

Moorman, Chick. *Where the Heart Is: Stories of Home and Family.* Saginaw, Mich.: Personal Power Press, 1996.

Nelsen, Jane, Lynn Lott, and H. Stephen Glenn. *Positive Discipline A-Z: 1001 Solutions to Everyday Parenting Problems.* Rocklin, Calif.: Prima Publishing, 1993.

Rutter, Virginia Beane. *Celebrating Girls: Nurturing and Empowering Our Daughters.* Berkeley, Calif.: Conari Press, 1996.

Wright, Esther. *Successful Parenting: Building Self-Esteem in Your Children.* Stillwater, Minn.: Greystone Educational Materials, 1994. 3-part video program.

Youngs, Bettie B. *How to Develop Self-Esteem in Your Child.* New York: Random House, 1993.

——————. *Stress and Your Child: Helping Kids Cope with the Strains and Pressures of Life.* New York: Random House, 1995.

Resource People

▼

The following list includes authors, consultants, trainers, parent educators and publishers—along with addresses, phone and fax information (where available) to help you contact them for additional information about their programs, services or resources.

Miriam Adderholdt-Elliot, Ph.D., Rt. 2, Box 470, Claremont, NC 28610. 704-547-2531.

Herb Anderson, 6606 Sundance Dr., Lincoln, NE 68512. 402-423-2605.

Kathie Baxter, Children's Small Press Collection, 719 N. 4th Ave., Ann Arbor, MI 48104. 1-800-221-8056.

Virgie Binford, Ph.D., 3027 Peabody La., Richmond, VA 23223. 804-780-7795.

Gus Blankenburg, Edumate Educational Materials, Inc., 2231 Morena Blvd., San Diego, CA 92110. 619-275-7117, fax 619-275-7120.

Jane Bluestein, Ph.D., ISS Publications, 1925 Juan Tabo NE, Suite B-249-H, Albuquerque, NM 87112. 1-800-688-1960, 505-323-9044, fax 505-323-9045.

Michele Borba, Ph.D., 840 Prescott Dr., Palm Springs, CA 92262. 619-323-5387, fax 619-323-5387.

Bev Bos, Turn the Page Press, 203 Baldwin Ave., Roseville, CA 95678. 916-782-6328.

Jack Canfield, Self-Esteem Seminars, P.O. Box 30880, Santa Barbara, CA 93131. 1-800-237-8336, 310-568-1505, fax 310-337-7465.

Jean Illsley Clark, 16535 9th Ave. N, Minneapolis, MN 55447. 612-473-1840.

Silvana Clark, Memory Makers, 3024 Haggin St., Bellingham, WA 98226. 360-734-9506, fax 360-734-9506.

Lynn Collins, Lynn Collins and Associates, 10205 San Gabriel NE, Albuquerque, NM 87111. 505-296-0009, fax 505-296-6638.

Barbara Coloroso, 3 Red Birch, Littleton, CO 80127. 303-972-3237.

Trudy Comba, Ph.D., Mahina Kai, Box 699, Anahola, HI 96703. 808-822-9451, fax 808-822-9451.

Joan Comeau, Ph.D., Family Information Services, 12565 Jefferson St. NE, Suite 102, Minneapolis, MN 55434-2102. 1-800-852-8112, 612-755-6233, fax 612-755-7355.

Elizabeth Crary, Parenting Press, Inc., 11065 5th Ave. NE, Seattle, WA 98125. 1-800-992-6657, 206-365-2900.

Deborah Critzer, Positive Parenting, 3067 Channel Drive, Ventura, CA 93003. 805-642-6384.

Morgan Daleo, Grace Publishing and Communications, P.O. Box 6629, Charlottesville, VA 22906-6629. 1-800-224-4617, fax 804-974-9931.

Orville Dean, 6640 Harris Road, Broadview Heights, OH 44147. 216-356-1634.

Mary Ann Dockstader, 909 Loma Verde Ave., Palo Alto, CA 94303. 415-494-6210.

Pat Dorff, Willow Tree Press, 8108 33rd Pl. N, Minneapolis, MN 55427. 612-546-4963.

Gail Dusa, P.O. Box 508, Gunnison, CO 81230. 303-694-4994, fax 303-694-4940.

Syndi Ecker, 6900 Llano, Atascadero, CA 93422. 805-466-6416, fax 805-549-8973.

Monte Elchoness, Ph.D., Monroe Press, 362 Maryville Ave., Ventura, CA 93003. 805-642-3064.

Jim Fay, 2207 Jackson Street, Golden, CO 80401. 1-800-338-4065.

LeRoy Foster, P.O. Box 65, Mt. Shasta, CA 96067. 916-926-2266, fax 916-926-3835.

Lynn Fox, Ph.D., 128 Sugarloaf Dr., Tiburon, CA 94920. 415-338-2265, fax 415-435-3992.

Dave Friedli, Toward a Drug-Free Nebraska, P.O. Box 2047, Hastings, NE 68902. 402-463-5611, fax 402-463-9555.

Trisha Gallagher, 301 Hollyhill Rd., Richboro, PA 18954. 215-364-1945.

H. Stephen Glenn, P.O. Box 788, Fair Oaks, CA 95628. 916-961-5556, fax 916-961-5570.

Chuck Glover, 4449 Ketcham Dr., Chesterfield, VA 23832. 804-745-4232, fax 804-648-6075.

Louis D. Gonzales, Ph.D., Center for Safe Schools, 14611 Wellington Rd., Minnetonka, MN 55391. 612-449-9877, fax 612-449-9877.

Jim Grant, 169 Grove St., P.O. Box 577, Peterborough, NH 03458. 603-924-9621, fax 603-924-6688.

Jean Haller, Journeys of Life, 810 Bellefonte St., Pittsburgh, PA 15232. 412-681-8755.

Merrill Harmin, Ph.D., 105 Lautner La., Edwardsville, IL 62026. 618-656-3173, fax 618-692-3359.

Suzanne Harrill, P.O. Box 270865, Houston, TX 77277-0865. 713-551-8284, fax 713-551-8284.

Louise Hart, Life/Skills Programs, P.O. Box 324, Boulder, CO 80306. 303-443-6105.

Stephen Haslam, Resource Associates, 4747 Bellaire Blvd., Suite 200, Bellaire, TX 77401. 713-661-3995, fax 713-661-3996.

J. D. Hawkins, 2000 N. Linden St. #C-02, Normal, IL 61761. 309-888-4511, fax 309-888-4912.

Bob Hoekstra, Team Architects, Inc., 1515 S. Orlando Ave. #X, Maitland, FL 32751. 407-740-6444, fax 407-740-0903.

Eve Hogan, 220 Oe St., Kihei, HI 96753. 808-879-0127.

Ann Holmes, Serenity Shop, 3401 San Mateo NE, Suite B, Albuquerque, NM 87110. 505-889-0885.

D. Trinidad Hunt, Elan Enterprises, 47-430 Hui Nene St., Kaneohe, HI 96744. 1-800-707-3526, 808-239-4431, fax 808-239-2482.

Ken Johnson, Ph.D., Turnpoint Publishing, P.O. Box 1251, Claremont, CA 91711. 909-626-2207.

Tim Jordan, M.D., 16120 Chesterfield Parkway S, Chesterfield, MO 63017. 314-530-7494.

MaryAnn Kohl, Bright Ring Publishing, P.O. Box 5768, Bellingham, WA 98227. 360-734-1601, fax 360-676-1271.

Kathryn Kvols, International Network of Children and Families, P.O. Box 7236, Gainesville, FL 32605. 1-800-257-9002, fax 352-338-3536.

Sr. Mary Alyce Lach, St. Norbert College, De Pere, WI 54115. 414-337-3063.

Clare LaMeres, Lifestyles Unlimited, P.O. Box 8326, Newport Beach, CA 92658. 714-854-2683.

Vicki Lansky, Practical Parenting, 15245 Minnetonka Blvd., Minnetonka, MN 55345. 612-912-0036, fax 612-912-0105.

Judy Lawrence, P.O. Box 13167, Albuquerque, NM 87112. 505-296-8792, fax 505-296-0632.

Beth K. Lefevre, Educational Systems Seminars, P.O. Box 1378, Boca Raton, FL 33429.

Ray Lemberg, Small Hands Press, 3337 N. Miller Rd., Suite 105, Scottsdale, AZ 85251. 602-994-9773.

Rokelle Lerner, 420 Summit Ave. #28, St. Paul, MN 55102. 612-227-4031.

Jeanne Lindsay, Morning Glory Press, Inc., 6595 San Haroldo Way, Buena Park, CA 90602. 714-828-1998.

Lulu Lopez, Ph.D., 1201 S. Eads St., Apt. 1509, Arlington, VA 22202. 703-892-5609.

Hanoch McCarty, Ph.D., Hanoch McCarty and Associates, P.O. Box 66, Galt, CA 95632. 1-800-231-7353, 209-745-2212, fax 209-745-2252.

Sandy McDaniel, Sandy McDaniel Enterprises, P.O. Box 15458, Newport Beach, CA 92659. 714-642-3605.

Bob Moawad, Edge Learning Institute, 2217 N. 30th #200, Tacoma, WA 98403. 253-272-3103, fax 253-572-2668.

Chick Moorman, Personal Power Press, Box 5985, Saginaw, MI 48603-0985. 517-791-3533, fax 517-791-6711.

Sherrill Musty, Waterfront Books, 85 Crescent Rd., Burlington, VT 05401. 802-658-7477, fax 802-658-7477.

Jane Nelsen, P.O. Box 788, Fair Oaks, CA 95628. 916-961-5551, fax 916-961-5570.

Marianna Nunes, 1746 Leavenworth St., San Francisco, CA 94109. 415-673-6775.

Herman Ohme, Ed.D., California Education Plan, 4185 Cherry Oak Pl., Palo Alto, CA 94306. 415-493-5512, fax 415-493-7604.

Susanna Palomares, Innerchoice Publishing, P.O. Box 2476, Spring Valley, CA 92077. 619-698-2437.

Rob Pennington, Resource Associates, 4747 Bellaire Blvd., Suite 200, Bellaire, TX 77401. 713-661-3995, fax 713-661-3996.

Evelyn Petersen, Parent Talk Productions, 843 S. Long Lake Rd., Traverse City, MI 49684. 616-943-9257.

Linda Pillsbury, Perspective Publishing, Inc., 50 S. Delacey St., Suite 201, Pasadena, CA 91105. 626-440-9635, fax 626-585-9441.

Aili Pogust, 238 Poplar, Marlton Lakes, NJ 08004. 609-753-0112.

Robert Reasoner, Self-Esteem Resources, 234 Montgomery La., Port Ludlow, WA 98365. 206-437-0300, fax 206-437-0300.

Sandi Redenbach, M.Ed., Esteem Seminar Programs and Publications, 313 Del Oro Ave., Davis, CA 95616. 1-800-354-6724, 916-756-8678, fax 916-756-5537.

Mike Smith, PSD, Inc., 3021 Mackland NE, Suite B, Albuquerque, NM 87106. 1-800-766-4546, 505-262-1187.

Gwynne Spencer, P.O. Box 30307, Albuquerque, NM 87190. Fax 505-268-4601.

Joey Tanner, Zephyr Press, 430 S. Essex La., Tucson, AZ 85711. 520-623-2022.

Tasneem Virani, Resource Associates, 4747 Bellaire Blvd., Suite 200, Bellaire, TX 77401. 713-661-3995, fax 713-661-3996.

Cynthia Whitham, 5164 Highland View Ave., Los Angeles, CA 90041. 213-259-9908.

Bruce Williamson, Back to Nurture, P.O. Box 398, La Honda, CA 94020. 415-747-0967.

Brad Winch Sr., Jalmar Press, 24426 S. Main St., Suite 702, Carson, CA 90745. 1-800-662-9662, 310-816-3085, fax 310-816-3092.

Bettie B. Youngs, Ph.D., Ed.D., Bettie B. Youngs and Associates, 3060 Racetrack View Dr., Del Mar, CA 92014. 619-481-6360, fax 619-481-8441.

List Index

▼

3 Ways to Deal with a Messy Room, 166

4 Ways in Which Boundaries Differ from Expectations, 72

4 Ways to Avoid Operating on a Double Standard, 232–233

4 Ways to Manage Your Anger, 246–247

5 Characteristics of a Good Boundary, 67–69

5 Criteria for Making Something Negotiable, 62–63

5 Reasons for Using Promises Instead of Threats, 79–80

5 Reasons to Help Your Children Learn to Express Their Feelings in Healthy, Nondestructive Ways, 199–200

6 Reasons *Not* to Ask Why, 77–78

6 Reasons *Not* to Give Your Child Advice, 159–160

6 Ways to Accommodate Your Child's Need for Control—Without Losing Control Yourself, 56–57

6 Ways to Take More Time for Yourself, 266–267

7 Characteristics of Families of Kids at Risk, 20–21

7 Choices You Can Offer at Bath Time, 167

7 Ways You Can Constructively Deal with Your Child's Abusive or Obnoxious Behavior, 241–242

8 Reasons Kids Rebel, 55

8 Things to Do When Your Child Makes a Mistake, 125–126

8 Things to Remember About Saying "I Love You," 105–106

8 Ways to Deal with Your Child's Saying "I Hate You!," 237–238

8 Ways to Model and Teach Gratitude, 41–42

9 Benefits of Asking Questions Instead of Giving Answers, 161–162

9 Characteristics of Good Listeners, 205–206

9 Characteristics of Responsible, Self-Managing Children, 9–11

9 Things to Remember When Setting a Boundary, 73–76

9 Things You Can Say to Detach from Unsolicited Advice or Criticism About Your Parenting Skills, 250–251

9 Ways to Be More Proactive, 230–231

9 Ways to Create Emotional Safety in Your Relationship with Your Child, 91–92

9 Ways to Minimize Problems with Homework, 145–147

10 Dangers of Encouraging Obedience and People-Pleasing, 22–24

10 Reasons to Offer Choices or Negotiate Options with Your Child, 60–61

10 Things to Remember About Changing Family Dynamics, 252–253

10 Things to Remember About Potty Training Your Child, 173–174

10 Ways to Avoid Getting Hooked by Your Child's Misbehavior, 239–240

10 Ways to Encourage an Appreciation for the Arts, 139–140

10 Ways to Encourage Responsibility, Independence and Self-Management, 12–14

10 Ways to Encourage Your Child's Individuality, 28–29

10 Ways to Make More Time for Your Child, 264–265

10 Ways to Minimize or Avoid Problems at the Grocery Store, 179–180

10 Ways to Respect Your Parents as Grandparents, 254–256

11 Reasons to Use Boundaries, 70–71

11 Things You Can Do to Build *Irresponsibility* in Your Child, 15–16

11 Ways to Avoid Problems over Money or Buying, 181–183

11 Ways to Create Success with Your Baby-Sitter, 186–188

11 Ways to Encourage Cooperation with Chores, 163–165

12 Reasons a Child May Want to Join a Gang, 95

12 Things *Never* to Say When Your Child's Feelings Have Been Hurt, 213–214

12 Things to Remember When You Offer Your Child Choices, 64–66

12 Ways to Avoid Problems at Bedtime, 168–169

12 Ways to Be an Effective Mentor, 5–6

12 Ways to Increase Positivity in Your Interactions, 107–109

12 Ways to Model Responsibility and Self-Discipline, 7–8

13 Arguments for *Not* Hitting Your Child, 243–245

13 Questions That Can Help You Learn from a Conflict with Your Child, 248–249

13 Things Kids May do to Create a Sense of Safety and Predictability in Their Lives, 93–94

13 Ways to Build Decision-Making Skills, 127–129

13 Ways to Help Your Child Deal with Death or Loss, 215–217

13 Ways to Model Respect, 32–33

14 Ways Parents Encourage People-Pleasing and Dependence, 25–27

14 Ways to Become a More Conscious Parent, 227–229

14 Ways to Create a Win-Win Home Environment, 51–54

14 Ways to Encourage a Lifelong Love of Learning, 118–120

14 Ways to Encourage Positive Choices for Good Health and Safety, 184–185

14 Ways to Help Your Child Deal with Monsters in the Closet, 170–172

14 Ways to Respect Your Child's Reality, 207–210

15 Characteristics of Children at Risk, 17–19

15 Negative or Hurtful Ways Kids Act Out Their Need for Power or Control, 58–59

15 Things to Remember About Reinforcing Positive Behavior, 110–113

15 Ways to Accommodate Your Child's Success Needs, 121–124

15 Ways to Drug-Proof Your Child, 192–194

15 Ways to Minimize Conflicts on Car Trips, 189–191

15 Ways to Model and Teach Optimism, 39–40

15 Ways to Model Self-Care, 43–45

16 Things You Can Suggest to Help Your Child Let Out Anger Nondestructively, 211–212

16 Ways to Avoid Conflicts over Food, 175–178

16 Ways to Model Courtesy, 30–31

17 Ways to Build Positive Relationships with Your Child's Teachers, 148–151

17 Ways to Build Tolerance, Compassion and Global Consciousness, 36–38

17 Ways to Help Your Children Survive Your Divorce, 218–221

17 Ways to Make It Safe for Your Child to Have and Express Feelings, 201–204

18 Characteristics of Parents at Risk, 234–236

18 of the Best Things About Having a Teenager in the Family, 261–263

18 Questions You Can Ask When Your Child Says "My Teacher Hates Me," 152–154

18 Things to Remember About Motivation, 81–85

19 Ways to Build Environmental Consciousness, 34–35

19 Ways to Build Thinking Skills, 130–134

22 of the Worst Things an Adult Ever Said to a Child, 100–101

23 Ways to Encourage Creativity and Imagination, 135–138

26 of the Best Things About Having Two-Year-Olds in Families, 257–260

26 Stress-Producing Obstacles in Relationships, 96–99

30 of the Best Things an Adult Ever Said to a Child, 102–104

31 Ways to Develop Literacy and a Love of Reading, 141–144

36 Things You Can Do to Feel Great!, 268–270

T

Things About My Parenting That I'm Really Proud Of, 275

Things I Hope My Children Have Learned from Me, 280

Things I Hope My Children Say About Me After I'm Gone, 276

Things I'm Willing to Change in My Own Behavior, 283

Things I Respect and Admire About My Children, 274

Things I've Done As Well As My Own Parents Did (in My Relationships with My Children), 278

Things I've Done Even Better Than My Own Parents Did (in My Relationships with My Children), 279

Things I've Done or Said That I Hope
   My Children Can Forgive, 281
Things I've Said That I Want My
   Children to Remember Forever, 273
Things I Would Like to Change in My
   Relationships with My Children,
   282

W
Ways I've Shown Love to My
   Children, 277

Subject Index

▼

A

abuse
  emotional. *see* emotional abuse
  physical. *see* physical abuse
  sexual. *see* sexual abuse
  verbal. *see* verbal abuse
abusive behavior, child's, 241–242
abusive language, 44, 58. *See also* verbal abuse
advice giving, 159–160
aggressiveness, 58
alcohol. *See* substance abuse
all-or-nothing thinking, 97
allowance, 181–182
anger
  child's, dealing with "I hate you!," 237–238
  giving child "space," 242
  nondestructive outlets, 211–212
  parental, managing, 246–247
arts appreciation, ways to encourage, 139–140
at-risk children, 3–4
  characteristics, 17–19
  family patterns, 20–21
at-risk parents, 234–236

attacking the problem and not the child, 91
attention-getting behaviors, 59, 239

B

baby-sitting success, 186–188
bath time resistance, overcoming, 167
bedtime problems, 168–169
behavior *vs.* worth, 107
blaming, 10, 20, 235. *See also* "victim talk"
boundaries
  following through once set, 71, 203–204
  "good" boundary characteristics, 67–69
  lack of, in at-risk homes, 20
  not asking "why" if child does not come through, 77–78
  reasons for setting, 70–71
  setting and expressing, 43, 53, 73–76, 91, 92
  setting when child is abusive, 241
  vs. expectations, 72
  vs. threats, 71, 74, 108
bribery *vs.* motivation. See under motivation

C

car-trip tips, 189–191
character building
    at-risk children, importance for,
        3–4
    modeling for your children, 3
children's rooms, messy, 166
choices, offering to children, 12, 56,
    60–61, 64–66, 81, 127
    food, 175
chores, 16
    breaking down into manageable
        units, 163
    "chore charts," 163
    cooperation building, 163–165
compassion, 36–38
compulsive eating. *See* eating disorders
conditional love, 21, 25, 106
conflict, fear of, 97
conflict management, 204, 248–249
conscious parenting, 227–229
consequences
    allowing child to experience, 13–14,
        57, 71, 129
    positive outcomes *vs.* punishment,
        108
contingencies, positive, 13, 68
control
    children acting out need for, 58–59
    child's needs *vs.* parents', 56–57
    stress-producing effects, 96
cooperation, 9, 12, 24, 53
courtesy, modeling for your children, 3,
    30–31
creativity, encouraging, 135–138
curiosity, ways to encourage, 136

D

death, helping child accept, 215–217
decision-making skills, 10, 13, 25, 52,
    127–129

dependence, 25–27. *See also* "people-
    pleasing"
depression in children, 217
developmental success, 121–124
divorce, helping child accept,
    218–221
double standards, 98, 232–233
drugs. *See* substance abuse

E

eating disorders, 58, 199. *See also* food
    conflicts
emotional abuse, 20, 100–101
emotional safety, 89–90, 91–92, 94
emotions, providing an outlet for your
    child's, 6. *See also* feelings
environmental consciousness, 34–35

F

fairness, 6
family change, 252–253
family dynamics, 252–253
family trees, 36
fear of failure, 18
feelings
    anger, nondestructive outlets,
        211–212
    child's reality, 207–210
    healthy expressions of, 199–200,
        201–204
    nondestructive outlets, 202
    poor responses to child with hurt
        feelings, 213–214
    "stuffed," 199–200, 204
    validation of, 202, 207, 208, 209,
        210, 216
    vs. behavior, 201
first-aid, 185
flexibility, 60
food conflicts, 175–178

G

gang activity, 95
global consciousness, 36–38
goals, parenting, 230, 254
goal setting, 124
grades, deliberately failing, 59
grandparenting, 254–256
gratitude, 41–42
grocery store struggles, 179–180

H

hitting child, 243–245
homework problems, minimizing,
    145–147
honesty, 6
humor, maintaining when dealing with
    your children, 109
hyperactivity, 217

I

idealizing child, 16
imaginary friends, 137
imagination. *See* creativity
independence, children, 13
individuality, encouraging in child,
    28–29
integrity, 6
intolerance, 20
irresponsibility, 15–16

J

journaling, 229

L

learning
    encouraging a love of, 118–120
    methods, 121
    styles of children, 146
listening to your child, 91, 201,
    205–206, 219, 228
loss, helping child accept, 215–217
lying, 15

M

manipulation by parents, 235
mentoring, 5–6
mistakes, helping child handle,
    125–126
modeling values for your children, 3, 6
    assertiveness, 193
    courtesy, 30–31
    drug use, 193
    environmental consciousness. *see*
        environmental consciousness
    gratitude, 41–42
    optimism, 39–40
    personal hygiene, 184
    positive health and safety choices,
        184
    reading, love of, 141–144
    respect, 32–33
    responsibility and self-discipline, 7
    self-care, 43–45
money issues, avoiding, 181–183
motivation
    choices, 81
    guilt or shame, 83
    meaningfulness, 83, 84, 113
    need-fulfilling, 82
    overmotivation, 84, 112
    positive, 233
    positive consequences *vs.* negative, 81
    self-sacrifice, 81–82
    tokens, 83
    vs. bribery, 84–85

N

name-calling, 33
negativity, 18, 40
negotiating, 62–63
nighttime fears, 169, 170–172

O

obedience, 22–24. *See also* "people-
    pleasing"

optimism, 39–40
overachievement, 18, 93
overidentification with children, 236
overmotivation. *See under* motivation

P
parental self-care, 225–226
  avoiding getting hooked into child's
    misbehavior, 239–240
  conscious parenting. *see* conscious
    parenting
  detaching from criticism of parent-
    ing skills, 250–251
  journal keeping, 229
  making time for yourself, 266–267
  managing parental anger, 246–247
  respecting own parents in grandpar-
    ent role, 254–256
  time for self, 229
  ways to help you feel great, 268–270
parenting, conscious. *See* conscious
  parenting
parenting, proactive. *See* proactive parenting
passive-aggressiveness, 23–24
peer pressure, 9
"people-pleasing," 9, 93, 110
  dangers if encouraged by parents,
    22–24
  ways parents encourage, 25–27
perfectionism, 18, 20, 44, 138
permissiveness, 50
personal hygiene, 184
physical abuse, 20, 58
positive affirmation statements,
  102–104
positive behavior reinforcement,
  110–113
potty training. *See* toilet training
power struggles
  avoiding, 49–50

food issues, 176
predictability
  importance to children, 89, 93–94
privacy
  children's need for, 32
proactive parenting, 230–231
problem solving, 50, 157–158
  baby-sitting, 186–188
  bath time resistance, 167
  bedtime resistance. *see* bedtime
    problems
  car trip conflicts, 189–191
  grocery store struggles, 179–180
  health and safety choices, 184
  money issues, 181–183
  question asking *vs.* answer giving,
    161–162
procrastination, 59
promises
  keeping, 8
  vs. threats, 53, 79–80

R
reading, importance of, 37, 38, 118,
  141–144, 228
rebellion, 94
  reasons kids rebel, 55
  as sign of child's need for control,
    58
respect
  modeling for your children, 3
responsibility, 6
  avoid overspending, 7
  at bedtime, 169
  characteristics of children who self-
    manage, 9–11
  encouraging in children, 12–14
  follow through on commitments, 7,
    68–69, 92
  homework, 145
  increasing child's level, 134

responsibility (*continued*)
  language, 8
  modeling, 7–8. *see also* modeling
    values for your children
  modeling for your children, 3
  promises, keeping, 8
  vs. building irresponsibility, 15–16
ridicule, 33
role models, 12

S

school participation, parents', 148
seat belt wearing, 184
self-care, 43–45
self-criticism, 18
self-discipline, 6
  modeling for your children, 3
self-harm
  child threatens to hurt himself, 59
selfishness, 45
self-management, 50, 52
self-mutilation, 94
self-righteousness, 20, 97
self-sacrifice, 82, 99
sexual abuse, 20
sexual activity, 94
shaming, 20, 83, 98, 126, 235
short-term goals, 25
skill building, 117
  learning. *see* learning
  practicing new skills, 122
  thinking. *see* thinking skills
smoking, 184, 199
sports, as alternative to drug use, 193
stress-producing relationship obstacles,
  96–99
study skills, 120
substance abuse, 9, 18, 20, 192–194, 199
supportiveness, 197–198
  stressed-out parents, 197
support network, 44

swearing, 58. *See also* verbal abuse

T

tantrums, 58
teachers
  building positive relationships,
    148–151
  child believes teacher is hostile,
    152–154
  conflict resolution, 149, 150, 151
teenagers, reasons to appreciate,
  261–263
television
  "allowance," 127
  educational, 119
  restricting, 144
testing limits, 55
thinking skills
  drug use, relationship between, 193
  games/toys requiring problem solv-
    ing, 131, 132
  helping child assess goals, 130
  increasing responsibility, 134
  open-ended questions, 130
  research tools, teaching child how to
    use, 133
  tactile stimulation, 132
  vocabulary development, 131
threats, 5
time management
  making more time for your kids,
    264–265
  making more time for yourself,
    266–267
toilet training, 173–174, 258
tolerance, 36–38
two-year olds, dispelling "terrible two"
  myth, 257–260

U

unconditional acceptance, 5

unconditional love, 12, 91, 105, 192
underachievement, 93

V

validating your child's reality, 5
validation, 202, 207, 208, 209, 210,
    216
verbal abuse, 20, 44, 58, 100–101,
    126
"victim talk," 8, 98
violence, 243

W

win-win solutions, 11, 50, 51–54, 242
    in boundary setting, 67–68, 70
    as prevention against drug use, 192
    vs. win-lose solutions, 54, 60
"write your own" lists
    things about my parenting that I'm
        really proud of, 275
    things I hope my children have
        learned from me, 280
    things I hope my children say about
        me after I'm gone, 276
    things I'm willing to change in my
        own behavior, 283
    things I respect and admire about
        my children, 274
    things I've done as well as my own
        parents did, 278
    things I've done even better than my
        own parents did, 279
    things I've done or said that I hope
        my children can forgive, 281
    things I've said I want my children
        to remember forever, 273
    things I would like to change in my
        relationships with my children,
        282
    ways I've shown love to my
        children, 277

About the Author

◆

D r. Bluestein has worked with parents for more than
20 years. A dynamic and entertaining speaker, she
has presented training programs to help build positive
adult-child relationships for parents, educators, counselors, health care professionals, military personnel and
other community members throughout the world. Her
down-to-earth speaking style, practicality and humorous stories and examples make her ideas clear and
accessible to a variety of audiences. She has appeared
internationally as a speaker and talk-show guest, including numerous appearances as a guest expert on *National
Public Radio, TalkNews Television, The David Brenner
Show, The Vicki! Show* and *The Oprah Winfrey Show.*

Dr. Bluestein is the author of *Parents, Teens &
Boundaries; Parents in a Pressure Cooker;* a set of
audiocassettes called *The Parent Tapes;* and a series of

booklets entitled *Proactive Parenting.* She has also written dozens of articles for magazines and resources such as *Family Information Services, Self Esteem Today, McCall's, Latina, Families in Recovery, B'Nai B'Rith Woman, The National Montessori, Offspring, Adolescence* and *PTA Today.* Her other books include *21st Century Discipline, Being a Successful Teacher* and the award-winning *Mentors, Masters & Mrs. MacGregor: Stories of Teachers Making a Difference.*

Dr. Bluestein was formerly a classroom teacher, crisis-intervention counselor and teacher educator. Currently, she heads Instructional Support Services, Inc., a consulting and resource firm that distributes resources for parents and educators, and provides staff development and parent training programs worldwide.

Dr. Bluestein can be reached at the following:

Jane Bluestein, Ph.D.
President
Instructional Support Services, Inc.
1925 Juan Tabo NE, Suite B-249
Albuquerque, NM 87112-3359
1-800-688-1960 • 505-323-9044 • fax 505-323-9045
e-mail to: jblue@wizrealm.com
http://wwwjanebluestein.com

New from the *Chicken Soup for the Soul* Series

Chicken Soup for the Teenage Soul

Teens welcome *Chicken Soup for the Teenage Soul* like a
good friend: one who understands their feelings, is there
for them when needed and cheers them up when things
are looking down. A wonderful gift for your teenage son,
daughter, grandchild, student, friend... #4630—$12.95

Chicken Soup for the Woman's Soul

The #1 *New York Times* bestseller guaranteed to inspire
women with wisdom and insights that are uniquely
feminine and always from the heart. #4150—$12.95

Chicken Soup for the Christian Soul

Chicken Soup for the Christian Soul is an inspiring reminder
that we are never alone or without hope, no matter how
challenging or difficult our life may seem. In God we find
hope, healing, comfort and love. #5017—$12.95

Chicken Soup for the Soul® Series

Each one of these inspiring *New York Times* bestsellers brings
you exceptional stories, tales and verses guaranteed to lift your
spirits, soothe your soul and warm your heart! A perfect gift
for anyone you love, including yourself!

A 4th Course of Chicken Soup for the Soul, #4592—$12.95
A 3rd Serving of Chicken Soup for the Soul, #3790—$12.95
A 2nd Helping of Chicken Soup for the Soul, #3316—$12.95
Chicken Soup for the Soul, #262X—$12.95

Selected books are also available in hardcover, large print,
audiocassette and compact disc.

Available in bookstores everywhere or call **1-800-441-5569** for Visa or
MasterCard orders. Prices do not include shipping and handling.
Your response code is **PBL**.